MERRITT & THE NICOLA VALLEY:
An
Illustrated History.

Nicola Valley Archives Association

Sonotek® Publishing
Merritt, B.C. Canada

Merritt & the Nicola Valley: An Illustrated History.

By the Nicola Valley Archives Association.

Book Project Team:
Monica McLeod, Krista Rocheleau, Daljit Dosanjh, Tracy Telles-Langdon, Tina Gilbertson.
Co-ordinator: Bette Sulz.

Canadian Cataloguing in Publication Data

Main entry under title:

Merritt & the Nicola Valley

   Includes bibliographical references.
   ISBN 0-929069-01-3

1. Nicola River Valley (B.C.) - History.
2. Merritt (B.C.) - History. I. Nicola Valley
Archives Association.
FC3845.N53M47 1989   971.1'72   C90-091017-8
F1089.N53M47 1989

ISBN 0-929069-01-3

Copyright © 1989

Nicola Valley Archives Association.
P.O. Box 1262,
2202 Jackson Avenue,
Merritt, B.C. Canada.   V0K 2B0

Published with the assistance of the British Columbia Heritage Trust.

SONOTEK® PUBLISHING P.O. Box 1752, Merritt, BC Canada V0K 2B0

Printed in Canada by Peerless Printers, Kamloops, B.C.

TABLE OF CONTENTS

Chapter One - Early Natives 1
Chapter Two - Brigade Trails 10
Chapter Three - Natives in Transition 14
Chapter Four - Early Settlers 20
Chapter Five - Settlements 26
Chapter Six - Merritt 32
Chapter Seven - Ranching 38
Chapter Eight - Mining 48
Chapter Nine - Logging 56
Chapter Ten - Transportation 62
Chapter Eleven - Hotels 70
Chapter Twelve - Schools 76
Chapter Thirteen - Public Services 82
Chapter Fourteen - Wars 88
Chapter Fifteen - Sports 92
Chapter Sixteen - Hunting/Fishing 96
Chapter Seventeen - Entertainment 98
Chapter Eighteen - Then & Now 104
Bibliography 106
Newspapers and Periodicals 106
Index 107
Map 115

Dedicated to the Pioneers of the Nicola Valley.

Foreword.

The Nicola Valley Archives Association (NVAA) is relatively new compared to many of the historical groups around the province of British Columbia. It was formed in the summer of 1976 and operated out of various temporary locations for five years before moving into a new Museum/Archives building at 2202 Jackson Avenue in Merritt. Although the Association had no "home" for its formative years, it made its presence known in the community through the publication of the *Nicola Valley Historical Quarterly*. This publication served to attract members from all over the world and hold the group together by providing a purpose for continuing research in the history of Merritt and the Nicola Valley.

While the *Quarterly* was largely text, the research revealed a broad selection of excellent photographs within the growing files of the NVAA and other collections, both private and public. Thus developed the idea to publish this book. It has taken half a dozen years plus countless hours of discussion and work—here are the results.

Acknowledgements.

Special thanks must go to: Pat Lean for his editing; Sigurd Teit for his photographs, valuable advice and many hours of assistance; Gerrard Guichon and Joe Lauder for their historical information and assistance in final proof-reading; Bette Sulz for her assistance in picture selection, layout, proof-reading and especially her support and encouragement; Ministry of Social Services and Housing, Employment Plus Program; to those whose photographs we chose to publish; and to everyone who submitted photographs for selection.

We are also indebted to present and past members of the book committee, especially Marie Logan, Margie Graham, Paula Collett, Bill Chaster, Doug Strand and Katharine and Murphy Shewchuk. Thanks also go to the past and present executive of the Nicola Valley Archives Association. Without their continuing support and encouragement, this book would not be a reality.

We wish to acknowledge the financial support of the Mayor and Council of the City of Merritt. We also take this opportunity to apologize for any acknowledgements we may have missed.

Monica McLeod, Krista Rocheleau, Daljit Dosanjh, Tracy Telles-Langdon and Tina Gilbertson.

1: EARLY NATIVES

The first people to inhabit the Nicola Valley were of the Interior Salish language group. These people made up the largest and strongest native group in British Columbia. The Thompson, Okanagan, Shuswap and Lillooet tribes were part of the Interior Salish family.

The Okanagan and Thompson tribes lived in the Nicola Valley. There is evidence that an Athapaskan-speaking tribe lived among the Salish at the end of the eighteenth century. By the early nineteenth century they were absorbed into the Salish family.

Fig. 1-1: Nicola Lake. -courtesy of Murphy Shewchuk.

The Native People's most difficult challenge was the provision of shelter, food and clothing.

Winter shelters, commonly called pit-houses or keekwillies, averaged eight to ten metres in diameter and approximately 1.5 metres deep. Construction was a family event usually completed in two days. Green timber was used for main posts with willow branches securing the braces and rafters. The whole structure was laced together with strips of bark and small boughs, layered with pine needles and grass, then covered with soil from the excavation. A notched pole served as a ladder at the entrance.

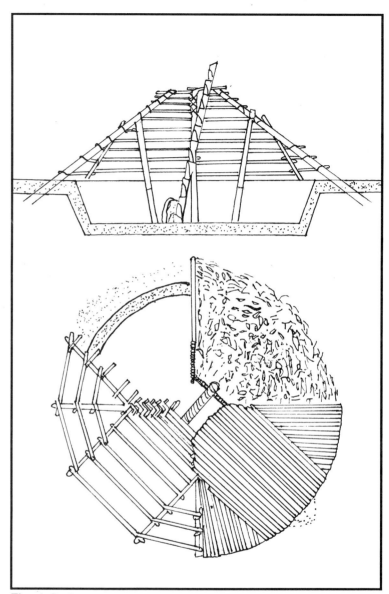

Fig. 1-3: Side and top views of winter shelter. Adapted by D. Dosanjh from "The Thompson Indians of B.C."

Fig. 1-2: A Nicola Valley Keekwillie (c.1898). -from the Dr. Sutton Album.

Summer shelters were usually circular in shape, ranging from five to six metres in diameter and six to seven metres in height. Long poles were leaned toward the center to form a conical shaped structure which was then covered with mats made of tule found in the vicinity. These shelters could be quickly taken down and moved from place to place. Sometimes the natives wintered in the shelters if they were located near their winter grounds. The conicals were reinforced for cold winter months with double layers of mat, banked with soil or bark and brush for insulation.

Fig. 1-4: Tule mats layered over the frame of a summer home. -by K.M. Rocheleau.

Fig. 1-5: Drying fish. -courtesy of NVAA.

Diet was determined by seasonal variations in food supply. The most important of all foods was salmon which was caught by means of spear, net, trap or weir.

During the salmon run native fishermen stationed themselves on boulders or ledges along the riverbanks and on larger rivers were secured by ropes to trees or rocks. Salmon were netted as they passed by or rested in the eddies, caught in dip-nets made of twine fastened on a wooden hoop attached to a long pole.

Fig. 1-7: Net fishing the Nicola River (c. 1900). -from the Dr. Sutton Album.

Fig. 1-6: A weir. -courtesy of the Geological Survey of Canada. #1063.

Weirs, fence-like structures, were constructed across smaller streams to stop ascending salmon. Openings were left leading to traps where salmon could be speared or raked out with gaff-hooks.

To preserve the salmon for winter, the meat was smoked or dried in the sun or over a fire.

Animal meat was also a valuable part of the diet and natives depended on deer and elk for food. Large animals were often killed by herding them to a chosen spot where they were shot by hunters lying in wait. Each carcass was skinned, cleaned, cut up, dried and stored for future use.

Berries, mushrooms and roots supplemented their dishes of fish and meat. Berries were eagerly gathered in season, spread on mats of woven rush to dry in the sun and then placed in storage baskets. Mushrooms and roots were dried by similar methods. Cooking preparation included steaming or boiling.

Strawberry Leather

Gather as many wild strawberries as you can.

Mash berries by hand or between two rocks.

Pour onto large chunks of cherry-bark.

Place these in the sun or on hot rocks and allow fruit to dry to a tough, leather-like consistency.

Peel the strawberry leather off the bark and store in a cool place.

It will keep well if thoroughly dried

Fig. 1-8: Strawberry Leather.

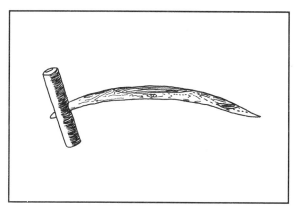

Fig. 1-9: Root digger made of serviceberry wood. -Drawing adapted by K.M. Rocheleau from "The Thompson Indians of B.C."

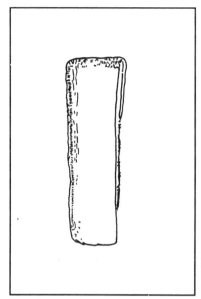

Fig. 1-10: Stone Axe

Tools, essential to their livelihood, were skilfully made of stone, wood, bark, bone or skins. Each of the many tools, having its special qualities, could be employed in more than one trade.

The axe and adze (not shown) took a prominent place among the stone implements. The axe head was a thick wedge with a groove near the top for securing a handle. Primarily used for domestic chores, it was also used along with fire for building canoes and felling trees.

Many uses of the knife made it indispensible for the natives daily chores and survival. Any material taking an edge was sharpened to make it effective for cutting, carving, scraping and various other purposes. Differences in material, weight and shape gave variety to the blade of sickle, dagger and scraper.

Fig. 1-12: Stone knife.

The arrow-flaker was made of antler. The large point was blunted and with a forward and downward pressure, flaked chips off arrowheads. The smaller point was sharpened for final stages of the work.

The wedge was a valuable tool for splitting and separating wood. The tapered, thin edge was usually made of stone or antler.

The skin-scraper, made from the foreleg bone or rib of a large animal, was one of the tools used to remove flesh from the hide.

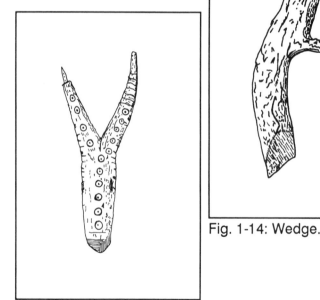

Fig. 1-11: Arrow Flaker.

Fig. 1-14: Wedge.

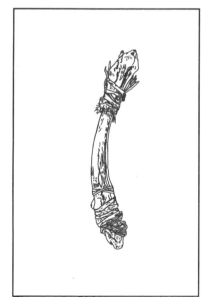

Fig. 1-13: Skin scraper.

Drawings adapted by K.M. Rocheleau from "The Thompson Indians of B.C."

Bows and arrows were used by natives for hunting and waging war. The one piece bow, usually made of juniper, was strengthened with cross wrappings of bird-cherry bark. The bow string of sinew was looped at one end and tied at the other. The arrow consisted of shaft, arrowhead and feathers. A special characteristic was the plummage ornamentation.

War arrowheads were loosely attached to the shaft so that they would remain in the wound, while hunting arrowheads were firmly secured, to be retrieved from the carcass later.

Tomahawks had broad, flat heads ending in a spike front with handles fastened with thongs. Shields and armor were worn for defence. Shields of wood and hide of elk or bear were made in a small, flat, circular shape. Armor vests were made of basket material or narrow strips of wood, or a tunic of elk hide might be worn entirely around the body. Weapons and armor were ornamented with horsehair, feathers, elk teeth and other adornment.

Fig. 1-17: Bow.

Fig. 1-15: Alexander KwikweiteskEt.(1910)
V.V. Vinson Photograph -courtesy of Sigurd Teit

Fig. 1-16: Spears and Bows (now in Peabody Museum) -courtesy of the Canadian Museum of Civilization, National Museums of Canada. #31007

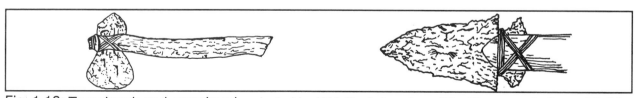

Fig. 1-18: Tomahawk and arrowhead. -adapted by K.M. Rocheleau from "The Thompson Indians of B.C."

Splendid basketry was one of the outstanding arts of the Interior Salish and was divided into three types, coiled, woven and bark.

Coiled baskets were made from cedar root splints, some had overlapping patterns of bleached grass and wild cherry bark and were distinguished by the unique designs of geometric, animal or other scenes. Sewing was done in a flat or ascending coil and the manner of applying stitches, either above, through, or under the foundation determined the shapes. Coiled baskets were made sufficiently water-tight that they were used for cooking pots.

Fig. 1-20: Basket maker. -Harry Priest photograph.

Fig. 1-19: Coiled Basket -courtesy of Murphy Shewchuk.

Woven basketry, in which the materials pass over and under one another were of many styles, checkerwork, twilled, wrapped and twined.

Birch bark baskets were made of bark that was cut into patterns, folded into shape, sewn with strips of willow and decorated with etched designs.

Basket weaving skills were used to make clothing, containers for harvesting, and most useful, pots, bowls and storage containers.

Fig. 1-21: Chief John Tetlenitsa (1910). V.V. Vinson Photograph -courtesy of Sigurd Teit

Tanned skin of the deer was generally used for clothing. Men wore shirts and breech cloths or trousers. Women wore undergarments, shirts, leggings and an overgarment which was either a dress or cape. Shirts similar in style, decorated with painted designs, interwoven horsehair or dyed porcupine quills, were worn by both men and women. The typical summer wear was made of light buckskin and woven sage bark. Heavier elk skin was used for winter clothing, which included trousers, shirts, coats, capes, hats, mitts and footwear. Ceremonial clothing was made more elaborate by ornamentation with quillwork and painted designs. Armlets, bracelets, belts and legbands accented the completed costume.

Fig. 1-23: Alice Roi.pellst. (1910) V.V. Vinson Photograph -courtesy of Sigurd Teit

Fig. 1-22: Left to Right: Sinsimtko Roi.pellst, Kwolalp (child), Chief Johnny Roi.pellst, Amy Roi.pellst (TEkwitlixkEn), and XaxalExkEn. (August 12, 1914). -courtesy of the Canadian Museum of Civilization, National Museums of Canada. #27000.

2: BRIGADE TRAILS

Early in January of 1813, Alexander Ross and his companion Jacques, fur traders with the Pacific Fur Company, left their recently established trading post at Cum Cloups (Kamloops) to return to their command post at Fort Okanagan.

Fig. 2-1: Alexander Ross. -courtesy of the British Columbia Archives and Records Service #HP4652

Fig. 2-2: Pack train on Tulameen Road. -courtesy of NVAA.

Fig. 2-3: Preparing to break camp.(c. 1900)
-photos on this page from the James Teit Album..

Fig. 2-4: Pack animals like Old Hessy (in photo) were essential for carrying supplies.(1901)

Fig. 2-5: Pack horses fording the river.(1901)

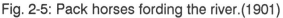

Ross decided to explore a part of the country he had never seen before. They trekked south over the mountains and eventually made their way into "a low and pleasant valley". Thus Ross and Jacques became the first white men known to enter the Nicola Valley. After a few days of rest from their arduous trip, they traded furs and, receiving directions from their native hosts, continued their journey to Fort Okanagan.

By 1827, Archibald McDonald, a clerk with the Hudson's Bay Company, had established a fur trade and good relations with Chief Nicholas of the Okanagan Salish Indians and approached him to help map the territory. It appears that McDonald drew his maps of the Nicola Valley through his knowledge of the Thompson River and information gained from Chief Nicholas and others.

The Oregon Treaty of 1846 established the 49th parallel as the boundary between American and British territories. Although the treaty allowed free navigation of the Columbia River, it created a new set of problems for the fur traders and a new route to the Pacific was essential. Alexander Caulfield Anderson, Chief Trader for the Hudson's Bay Company, was given permission to search for an all British route for the fur brigades. He made several attempts to reach Kamloops from Hope via the Coquihalla River, Boston Bar Creek and the Nicola Valley, but failed.

In 1849, Anderson settled on a trail explored earlier by Henry Peers. Leaving the Fraser at Fort Hope, Anderson headed almost due east up the Coquihalla River. The trail followed the river upstream to the junction of Peers Creek, Sowoqua Creek, down Podunk Creek and across the Tulameen River. It then followed an old Indian trail across Lodestone Mountain to the Otter Creek Valley and north into the Nicola watershed near Aspen Grove. From there the trail went along the west side of Quilchena Creek to Nicola Lake through the open grasslands, before continuing up and out of the valley near Napier Lake. The trail then angled west near Brigade and McLeod Lakes and into the Thompson Valley at Kamloops. Commercial use of Anderson's Trail through the Nicola Valley continued until the 1860s.

Fig. 2-6: Alexander Caulfield Anderson. -courtesy of the British Columbia Archives and Records Service #HP2228.

Fig. 2-7: "Geoffry Lodwick cinching up pack with Gutherie's help."

In Hudsons Bay Company terms, an "express" was a party travelling lightly, carrying mail but no freight. The heavily loaded parties bringing out furs or carrying other freight were termed "brigades".

The brigades brought the furs to the coast in the spring and took back trade goods and supplies to the interior trading posts on their return trip. On the outgoing trip, the horses were each loaded with two 80 pound bails of furs with some of the brigades numbering more than 200 horses.

Fig. 2-9: Cowboy

Fig. 2-8: The terrain was rugged and the risks were high. Here one of the pack horses has fallen off the trail and into the river.
-photos courtesy of NVAA.

3: NATIVES IN TRANSITION

The earlier explorers who travelled to the Northwest through the valley did not have much effect on the natives until Chief Nicola became involved with trade goods. Fur traders from Thompson's River Post encouraged the natives to abandon their hunting and fishing in favor of trapping.

Fig. 3-1: An Old Timer of the Nicola Valley. (c.1920) -Harry Priest photograph.

Fig. 3-2: Jenny and papoose. (c.1900) -from the Dr. Sutton Album.

Low fur prices and overtrapping the area left the natives depen-dant on trade goods which resulted in a marked change in their lives. By 1868, white men began settling in the Nicola Lake area. With this encroachment came the first Indian reserves; one was located at the northeast end of Nicola Lake and a fishing reserve was established to the south of the lake.

By 1871, when British Columbia joined Canada, settlers and missionaries had established several communities in the valley.

Fig. 3-4: A family photo. -courtesy of NVAA.

Fig. 3-3: Shulus Reserve cowboys. (c.1900) -from the Dr. Sutton Album.

Disagreements arose between natives and settlers as to who had claim to the land. In 1878, after negotiations, two more reserves were assigned on separate sites near Douglas Lake. That same year three reserves were established in the Chapperon Lake area east of Douglas Lake.

Fig. 3-5: Father Le Jeune.
-courtesy of NVAA.

Arriving in 1882 Father Le Jeune, a Catholic Missionery Priest, quickly became known for his teachings. He was involved in construction of the first churches built at Coldwater Reserve (1885), Douglas Lake (1888), and Nicola Lake Indian Reserve (three miles east of Quilchena).

In 1905, Fr. Le Jeune opened a church at Shulus and he dedicated the first Catholic Church in Merritt in 1911. He continued to serve the native people of the valley until 1927.

Fig. 3-6: Nicola Valley natives. (c.1910) -Harry Priest photograph.

Fig. 3-7: Pankute, one of the old hunters. (c.1898) -from the Dr. Sutton Album.

Unchained Horizons

To be one,
        given three
I am — the soft darkness
        of my eyes

        — memories
                protected memories

Days of softness, leaning on my mother's knee,
running in the fields — laughing.
See the eagle, my hands reaching,
it drops a feather to me.
To the top of the hill climbing, climbing
and I reach it — and now
I am — into the years
        of my life

Fig. 3-9: -photos courtesy of NVAA

        — today.
Here today, I pause in the midst of changes.
A new beginning with different colours, different feelings.
The steel blue sky holds my steady gaze to the boundaries
of the horizon. The emerald green of grass
is now the trodden trails, thoughts made visible
to the repetition of destination.   Listen, hear the wind?
I lift my head and brush my weathered brow,
proudly and unfaultering, make new paths
              — for new ways — until
I am — again, the majestic spirit
                  cradled in the wind.
Freedom,
        eternal freedom
as my spirtit roams the hills.
The spring with fragrant buttercups lingers
into summer. The rainbow carpet over the soft warm earth
surrenders to autum's golden harvest,
winter spreads an ermin, and as it covers the land
I know this is heaven — and I never want to leave again.

by Monica McLeod.

Fig. 3-8:

A lthough the natives retained many of their old beliefs and customs, most of their social and economic systems changed.

Fig. 3-10: Mealtime. (c.1898) -from the Dr. Sutton Album.

4: EARLY SETTLERS

Fig. 4-1: Left to Right: John Clapperton (first postmaster and government agent), George Clapperton (father of distinguished locomotive engineer "Smokey"), William Voght ("Father of Merritt") and Thomas Carrington (pioneer merchant). -courtesy of Allan & Gloria Collett.

The Nicola Valley, nestled between bunchgrass covered hills and rolling mountains, and known only to natives and a few white men now attracted hardy pioneers.

First, Edwin Dalley, born in Southern England, made his way to the valley in April of 1868 where he pre-empted land at the foot of Nicola Lake. With him came Alexander Robb, representing John Clapperton and on his behalf pre-empted land next to Dalley's. Later John Clapperton and Edwin Dalley, who had formerly been shipmates, entered into a partnership raising sheep.

When John Clapperton took up residence on his pre-emption, Robb entered land at the mouth of Quilchena Creek. Brothers Florien and Wheeler Mickle settled on land to the north of Alexander Robb.

Fig. 4-2: Edwin Dalley's homestead. -courtesy of NVAA

Fig. 4-3: Mr. & Mrs. Wheeler Mickle. -courtesy of Johnny Potts

Fig. 4-4: Joseph and Violette Moore. -photos courtesy of NVAA

Samuel and John Pearcy Moore settled at the head of Nicola Lake on July 1, 1868. There they started Beaver Ranch which later became a family venture. The youngest brother, Joseph joined them in 1871, followed by parents Margaret and John Sr. in 1872. With them was the fourth brother, Benjamin.

The years 1869 - 1871 brought Richard W. Turner to Douglas Lake; John Gilmore, Robert Lettice and George Clapperton to Nicola Lake, George Muir and James Chapman to Forks of Nicola (Merritt); Harvey Woodward and brother Thomas to Nicola Valley (Lower Nicola) and Henry Lindley to Potatoes Illahie (14 Mile).

Fig. 4-5: Samuel Moore.

Fig. 4-6: John Moore.

Fig. 4-7: Sam and Matilda Moore.

Fig, 4-8: Thomas Woodward, Father of Marcus Woodward. -courtesy of NVAA.

In the winter of 1871, brothers William and John Charters settled in the Nicola Valley. William at the south end and John northwest of what is now Merritt. Today John rests peacefully at the Murray United Church Cemetery at Nicola along with Samuel Moore, Florin Mickle and others.

Jesus Garcia, born in 1832 in Sonora, Mexico, first entered the valley in the 1860s on his way to the Cariboo goldfields with supplies for miners. He spent the winters pasturing his pack animals in the Nicola Valley. In 1872 he settled on land adjacent to William and John Charters' properties.

Other settlers who arrived in 1872 were Byron Earnshaw (Canford), Thomas Carrington (Lower Nicola), Joseph Blackbourn (Quilchena) and A.W. Lundbaum (Nicola Lake).

Fig. 4-9: A gravestone at the Murry Church Cemetery. -courtesy of Murphy Shewchuk.

Fig. 4-10: Marcus and Sarah Woodward
-photos courtesy of NVAA.

In 1873, William Palmer, Martin Stemwick, Patrick Ryan and Robert Hamilton moved to the Nicola Valley. Thomas and Harvey Woodward were joined by their brother Marcus. William Voght, of German ancestry, moved to the valley during the summer and took up land previously held by George Muir who had drowned earlier that spring. Joseph Guichon was first to pre-empt land at Mamette Lake. Alexander Coutlie (original spelling), a native of Quebec, arrived to take up land west of "The Forks" where he developed a commercial centre known as Coutlee.

Fig. 4-11: Joseph Guichion.

Fig. 4-12:
Some of those who attended the Alexander Coutlie funeral January 6, 1901 were:

1. Del King	2. Alf Godison	3. Henry S. Cleasby
4. Alfred Collett	5. Johnny Wilson	6. George Bent
7. Charles M. Newkirk	8. Thomas Curnow	9. Thomas Swarts
10. James M. Smith	11. Sandy Swan	12. Albert E. Howse
13. L.B. McGregor	14. Jesus Garcia	15. Marcus Woodward
16. William Charters	17. James Chapman	18. Jack Clark
19. Joseph Smulot	20. William Voght	21. George B. Armstrong
22. Alex Gordon	-sketch by K.M. Rocheleau.	

Fig. 4-13: Alexander Coutlie funeral. -1901- -courtesy of NVAA.

5: SETTLEMENTS

Fig. 5-1: Nicola Settlement. (c.1899) -courtesy of NVAA.

Settlements followed the pre-emptions and from the mid 1870s to the turn of the century small rival communities started to take shape. The race was on to see which community would become the major center of the valley.

The first post office in the valley opened at Nicola Lake in 1871. John Clapperton was postmaster and Justice of the Peace. In 1872, George Petit grew the first wheat and George Fensom built the first grist mill at Mill Creek. Fensom also built John Clapperton's grist mill at Nicola Lake which was operated by Robert Lettice. By 1882, the community of Nicola Lake, (shortened to "Nicola" in 1905) was the government and commercial center of the valley.

Fig. 5-3: Nicola Courthouse.-courtesy of NVAA.

Fig. 5-2: John Clapperton. -courtesy of the British Columbia Archives and Records Service #HP5172.

At Nicola Lake, George Petit opened the first general store which was later sold to Indian Agent, A.E. Howse. The first Court House was built in 1884 at the cost of $517.00. Howse brought in the first steam sawmill in 1887, built the first roller mill in 1890 and owned and operated the Driard Hotel. Barwick & Co. had the harness and saddlery shop and after the turn of the century William Pooley built the Pooley Hall. Joseph Dixon Lauder, who had arrived in 1876, succeeded Clapperton in 1899 as government agent. Lauder was also magistrate, tax assessor and collector.

Fig. 5-4: Joseph Dixon Lauder. -courtesy of the British Columbia Archives and Records Service. #HP72116.

Fig. 5-5: Nicola's main street. Next to Barwick's was the hall and A.R. Carrington's Shop which included the post office. (c.1900) -from the Dr. Sutton Album.

Quilchena, north of Nicola, had R. Johnson as its first storekeeper and postmaster. He sold to W.R. Megaw who later sold to Robert Charters in 1885. Charters ran the store and post office for many years. After several ownership changes Quilchena store was sold to the Guichons. Other businesses at Quilchena were a community hall, Joseph Blackbourn's hotel, Edward O'Rourke's general store, Richard O'Rourke's blacksmith shop, and Doctor Michael MacMahon Murphy.

Due south of Nicola is Aspen Grove, situated on the divide between the Similkameen and Nicola Valleys. A country store here has served ranchers, prospectors and miners for many years. The earliest record of the Aspen Grove post office is September, 1901.

Fig. 5-6: The Quilchena Store, the first building in the valley constructed of stone, was built by the Guichons in 1912. -courtesy of Guy Rose.

Fig. 5-7: Aspen Grove Store. -courtesy of NVAA.

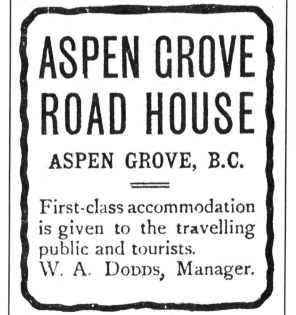

ASPEN GROVE ROAD HOUSE

ASPEN GROVE, B.C.

First-class accommodation is given to the travelling public and tourists.

W. A. Dodds, Manager.

Fig. 5-8: -Advertisement in the Nicola Herald. (April 2, 1909.)

Northwest of The Forks, where the valley narrows, is the settlement of Coutlee. In 1873, Alexander Coutlie built a house here and obtained a licence to sell liquor. In the early 1880s, he built a hotel, store and warehouse. The post office operated out of this store from 1885 to 1917.

Blair and Company and Coutlee's Blacksmith Shop also served the needs of the area from this community.

Fig. 5-9: Coutlee. (c.1900) -from the Dr. Sutton Album.

The Woodward family was greatly involved in the settlement at Lower Nicola. Marcus Woodward owned the general store and mill and was the community's second postmaster. His brother Melvin taught school there from the last month of the 1876 school year to March of the following year. Queenie Woodward, a dog, was registered because low enrollment threatened closure of the school. In 1889, G.B. Armstrong built his first store at Lower Nicola. James M. Smith owned and operated the blacksmith shop.

Northwest of Lower Nicola was John Manning's 21-Mile Ranch, Alex Gordon's 22-Mile House, and at the mouth of the Nicola River, Richard Curnow owned and operated another stopping place.

Fig. 5-10: Melvin Woodward. -courtesy of NVAA.

Fig. 5-11: Canford General Store in the early 1920s. Preparing to pack in to a forest fire. -courtesy of NVAA.

Page 31

6: MERRITT

Three ranches, owned by William Voght, Jesus Garcia and the John Charters estate, at the confluence of the Nicola and Coldwater Rivers became the focus of a farming community known as "The Forks" in the 1880s. With the completion of the C.P.R. through British Columbia in 1885, interest increased in the coal deposits south of The Forks.

Part of the ranches owned by Voght, Garcia and Charters was surveyed in 1893 for the townsite of Forksdale, but the name did not stick. Instead, the name was changed to Merritt in 1906 to honor William Hamilton Merritt, a mining engineer and railway promoter. By 1907, the coal mines were in operation. With the completion of the railway from Spences Bridge, government and other offices started moving from Nicola to establish Merritt as the major settlement in the valley.

Fig. 6-1: The corner of Quilchena Avenue and Voght Street in Merritt. Frank Garcia waiting to pick up parcels for Aspen Grove using Alex Coutlie's wagon and team. -courtesy of NVAA.

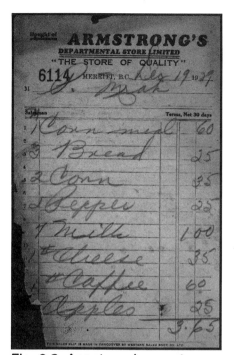

Fig. 6-2: Armstrong's counter bill. -courtesy of George Armstrong.

Armstrong's Store moved from Lower Nicola to Nicola Avenue, Merritt in the spring of 1907. G.B. Armstrong became Merritt's first postmaster at this location in 1908. In 1910, Armstrong's Departmental Store moved to 2025 Quilchena Avenue.

In 1909, the Bank of Montreal moved from Nicola to Merritt. A.E. Howse moved his department store to the west end of Nicola Avenue. The Nicola Herald, founded at Nicola Lake in 1905, moved from Nicola to Merritt in 1909 and the name changed to the Merritt Herald and Nicola Valley Advocate.

Other industries developed in the valley, including ranching, copper mining and lumbering. As a result, new business buildings were constructed.

H. PRIEST, Photographer
MERRITT, - - B.C.

Fig. 6-5: H. Priest, Photographer. -from the Nicola Herald, April 2, 1909.

Fig. 6-4: Harry Priest. His well-known photography captured the excitement and history of the Nicola Valley and its people from his arrival in 1909 until the mid 1940s. -courtesy of the Moffats.

Fig. 6-3: Armstrong's Departmental Store on Quilchena Avenue. Merritt New year 1921. -courtesy of G. Armstrong.

Fig. 6-6: William Hamilton Merritt.
-courtesy of NVAA.

The move towards incorporation began in 1910 and culminated when, on April 1, 1911, Merritt was granted its city charter.

Merritt City Hall was built in 1912. The top floor was headquarters for police, the second for administration offices, and the bottom for the jail. It included a tower which housed a whistle to summon the volunteer fire brigade.

Merritt dedicated names of streets to early settlers: Charters, Chapman, Cleasby, Garcia, Voght; and avenues to communities: Coutlee, Nicola, Granite and Quilchena.

Fig. 6-7: Merritt City Hall. (Circa 1930.)
-courtesy of NVAA.

Fig. 6-8: **FIRST CITY COUNCIL (1911) CITY OF MERRITT**   -courtesy of NVAA.

Back Row: Ald. P. Boyd, Ald. D. Munro, Ald. N. McMillan, Mayor I. Eastwood, Ald. F.A. Reid, Ald. J.A. Menzies, Ald. A. Jackson.

Front Row: (seated) City Clerk H. Priest, City Solicitor M.L. Grimmett.

Even before his death, William Henry Voght was known as "the Father of Merritt". His relentless pursuit of development and his dedication to the valley and its people remained with him to his death on February 4, 1911.

Fig. 6-9: William Voght. -courtesy of NVAA.

Fig. 6-10: Diamondvale Store: present Super-Valu parking lot.
-courtesy of British Columbia Archives and Records Service. #HP73154.

Fig. 6-11: Merritt Courthouse, located on Nicola Avenue.
-courtesy of Merritt Herald.

As the town grew Mr. Rankin opened a drug store, Menzies a general store and Simpson and Cranna a jewellery store. Merritt Brewery was located at the corner of Spring Street and Granite Avenue. The first electrical power service by the city of Merritt was provided in February 1913.

Merritt and the Nicola Valley experienced prosperity until the passage of restrictive trade legislation in the U.S.A. in 1930. Because Merritt had financially backed one of the major sawmills, the loss of lumber markets caused the city to go into receivership from 1933 until 1952.

Fig. 6-15: 1906-1912 brand. -courtesy of NVAA.

Fig. 6-12: Simpson & Cranna, Elgin pocket watch. -courtesy of Gordon Heslop.

Fig. 6-14: The Merritt Post Office was completed in 1943. Mr. Charlie Isitt, Mrs. Isitt and Mr. Battersby are in this photograph. -Harry Priest photograph.

Fig. 6-13: The Bank of Montreal, post office and dentist office were located in the (Archie) Jackson Building. (Photo taken in 1912. Now known as Post Meat Market.) -courtesy of NVAA.

7: RANCHING

The end of the Cariboo gold rush and the beginning of the construction of the Canadian Pacific Railway brought the beginning of the ranching era in the Nicola Valley. The fine native grasses became prime feed for 'gold on the hoof'.

The demand by lower mainland merchants for Interior beef prompted the construction of the Coquihalla Trail from Hope to Nicola in 1876. This remained the main route to the coast until it was replaced by wagon roads to the C.P.R. shipping points at Spences Bridge and Kamloops in 1885. In 1907, the CPR built a line from Spences Bridge to Nicola Lake. This created a direct outlet for cattle shipments and increased ranching opportunities.

Fig. 7-1: Early homesteading in the Nicola Valley. (c.1900) -from the Dr. Sutton Album.

Beginning in the 1870s, many ranches, unable to operate on a small scale, were bought by larger ones such as the Douglas Lake Cattle Company, founded by Joseph Blackbourne Greaves, Charles M. Beak, Charles W. Thomson and William C. Ward in 1886. The "hundred and eleven" (111) brand registered by Beak has become as famous as the Douglas Lake Cattle Company, now solely owned by Charles N. Woodward.

The Rey Ranch at Mamette Lake, originally homesteaded by Pierre and Joseph Guichon, is now owned by the Garthwaites. Their other properties include the neighbouring Wilbur and Henry Davis Ranch (the former Quinville pre-emption).

Before the turn of the century the Guichon family moved from Mamette Lake to Chapperon Lake, then to Nicola Lake. After 1900, many small and large ranches were added to the Guichon holdings including the Beaver Ranch of the Moore family at the head of Nicola Lake, and the hotel and general store at Quilchena. In 1957, the Guichon holdings were divided between Gerard Guichon (north sections) and Guy Rose (south sections), descendants of founder Joseph Guichon

The Hamilton Brothers, John, Robert, and Jim, were well known for horse breeding. The Hamilton brothers left the valley in the 1880s to ranch in the Calgary, Alberta area.

Fig. 7-2: Joseph Blackbourne Greaves. -courtesy of Nina & Neil Woolliams.

Fig. 7-3: Douglas Lake Cattle Company (home ranch.) 1947-48 -courtesy of Vern Ellingson.

Fig. 7-4: Johnny Guichon (far right) on his way to the cow camp at Courtney Lake. -courtesy of NVAA.

Fig. 7-5: Courtney Lake Cow Camp (1948).
-courtesy of Vern Ellingson.

When he died, Alexander Coutlie's property was sold to long-time employee, Harry Cleasby. Across the Coldwater River from Coutlee, land pre-empted by James Chapman was sold to John H. Collett in 1906.

Fig. 7-6: LEFT to RIGHT: ?, Fred Shrimpton, Jack Collett, Dick Curnow, Harry Collett, Tom Curnow and Leslie Curnow at the Collett Ranch. (June, 1941.)
-courtesy of Dennis Curnow.

Fig. 7-8: Blondie Ellingson (on horse), Herman Earnshaw and George Sickmen (driving). -courtesy of Vern Ellingson.

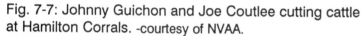

Fig. 7-7: Johnny Guichon and Joe Coutlee cutting cattle at Hamilton Corrals. -courtesy of NVAA.

The Lauder Ranch at Quilchena, pre-empted by Joseph Dixon Lauder, was acquired by William H. Lauder in 1903 when his father retired. This ranch, now in the fourth generation, was recently turned over to John Lauder, son of Joseph William (Joe).

The original Pooley Ranch, east of Merritt, was purchased by William Pooley in 1881. William's cousin, Jim, arrived in 1885 and settled on a ranch adjacent to his. Jim became involved in the sheep business until his lease ran out. He then took up ranching in the Coyote Valley area. In 1911, Jim Pooley was killed. His brother William John arrived from England in 1912 to take over the ranch. William's descendants still operate Pooley Ranch.

Steffens Ranch, seven miles south of Mamette Lake, was pre-empted by Henry (Harry) Steffens in 1904. After his death in 1910 the ranch was passed to his sons, Harry, Rupert, Fred, Jim, Tom, Carroll, Frank and Dick. The brothers, except Harry who never lived on the ranch, ran it for several years. It became known as the Steffens Bros. or 7B Ranch. Today, this original ranch is owned by Jim Steffens, grandson of Henry Steffens.

Two long-time ranches of Lower Nicola recently sold; Gardner's (pre-empted by the Woodwards) to Robinson Brother's Farm and Capp's to Fritz Ludwig.

It is interesting to note that the properties of William Voght, John Charters, and William Charters from which the first town lots were subdivided are now completely within the city of Merritt. Only a part of Jesus Garcia's lot 123 is still being used for ranching.

Fig. 7-9: Left to Right: Lloyd Barrett, Vernon Corkle, Jack Morrissey, Geoff Curnow, Joe Lauder and Gordon Curnow. Taken in front of old house, Lauder Ranch (Merritt), now known as River Ranch. (c.1934). -courtesy of Joe Lauder.

Fig. 7-10: Alice and William John Pooley on original homestead. -courtesy of NVAA.

Fig. 7-11: Douglas Lake Ranch Cattle Drive (1976).
-courtesy of Murphy Shewchuk.

Fig. 7-12:
Joe Coutlee and Harry Charters. Douglas Lake,
1932.-courtesy of Frank Archer.

Fig. 7-13:
Dolores and Norman
(Scotty) McLeod.
-courtesy of M. McLeod.

Of the many ranches of the Aspen Grove area all but two became part of the Douglas Lake Cattle Company. McLeod Ranch, is now owned by Gordon, previously owned by his parents Dolores and Norman (Scotty) McLeod and Willow Heights Ranch is owned by Nellie and Leslie J. Bryant.

The market for horses was good until the 1940s when horses were replaced by tractors and other vehicles.

Fig. 7-14: Saddling a wild horse. Ranger Coutlee (end of rope), Harry Collett (at fence), and Jackie Walters (sitting on fence). -courtesy of Gloria & Allan Collett.

Fig. 7-15: Ben Fink in his brand new $15.00 outfit. (1934-35) -courtesy of NVAA.

Fig. 7-16: Ed Tillery seated on mower during hay cutting at Dodd's place, Aspen Grove, during World War I. -courtesy of NVAA.

Ranchers originally depended on native grasses for winter feed, but after several severe winters they started stacking hay. Pitchforks and wagons were first used to gather cut hay from fields. Later, hay production meant spring plowing, seeding and clearing irrigation ditches. Flood-irrigating hay lands took about six weeks. Mowing, raking and other operations usually required a two-horse team for each rig. Stackers completed the harvest and fenced in the hay stacks.

In one method of stacking, hay was brought from the field with a bull rake, lowered onto slings then lifted with a frame, pulleys and ropes. Sling ropes were pulled by horses until the hay could be dropped on top of the stack.

Fig. 7-18: Guichons stacking hay by pulley. -courtesy of Gerard Guichon.

Fig. 7-17: Frank Archer on hay rake. -courtesy of Frank Archer.

Page 44

Fig. 7-19: Harvesting a field of oats at Douglas Lake. -courtesy of Bill Huxley.

Over the years gradual changes in cattle ranching have included the implementation of the Grazing Act, improved methods of clearing land, better irrigation and water power systems. Modernization continues with new equipment, improved communications and management. Changes adopted in livestock breeding, and marketing methods affect production and are an essential part of progress and survival of ranching.

Fig. 7-20: Bill Gillespie, Guichon shepherd. -courtesy of V. Elischuck.

Fig. 7-22: Joe Cleasby, H. Cleasby, Sam Gerrard and Mr. Eastwood at Coutlee's N.V. Meat Market Piggery. -courtesy of NVAA.

Fig. 7-21:　Heron brothers' sheep. (One of three bands with about 3,000 sheep in each band.) -courtesy of Ron Bevan.

Attempts were made at pig ranching, but it was found that pork could be imported at less cost than raising it.

Sheep ranching was common in the valley from the earliest settlers to the mid 1950s. Sheep ranchers included the Capps, Gillises, Guichons, Pooleys, Thompsons and Bob, Jim and Tom Heron. The Heron brothers were in business for 24 years and owned the largest flock. Their sheep range included the Stoyoma Mountain, Hooshum Ridge and Murray Lake areas.

Fox farming began in 1913 in Lower Nicola. The Merritt Fox Ranch, largest fox ranch in the valley, was owned by Dr. J.J. Gillis and operated by Charles and Edgar Collett. When Dr. Gillis started fox ranching he arranged for a shipment of twenty pairs of foxes from his brother in P.E.I. Some other breeders in the valley were A.E. Axten, W. Crompton, J. Guichon, Mrs. Marshall, Issac Millar and Mrs. Eric Gavelin.

Fox farming was a profitable business until the Second World War and then was quickly phased out.

Fig. 7-23: Cat and Silver Fox cubs -Harry Priest photograph.

Fig. 7-24: Lake View Fox Pelts -Harry Priest photograph.

Fig. 7-25: Nicola Valley Silver Fox Company -courtesy of NVAA.

8: MINING

It is known that coal from the Nicola Valley was "exported" by packhorse to the blacksmiths at Clinton as early as 1869 and may have been taken by local natives to Lytton during the Cariboo Gold Rush. Early settlers mined coal from surface outcroppings to fuel their fires. In 1904, John Hendry staked 2700 acres of coal rights.

Fig. 8-1: Mr. Kinny (far left) at Aberdeen Camp. (c.1900) -from the Dr. Sutton Album.

A survey by Dr. Ellis, a geologist, in 1904 revealed large coal deposits in the region and, as a result, interest increased. The CPR took over William H. Merritt's railway charter in 1905. Work then commenced on a railroad from Spences Bridge to Nicola and development of coal properties began. In 1906, Coal Gulley, one of the first coal companies in production, was taken over by Nicola Coal and Coke Company. Shortly after, several other coal properties started development including Coldwater Coal Co. and Diamondvale Coal and Iron Mines Ltd.

Nicola Valley Coal & Coke Co.'s. No. 1 Tipple. Middlesboro, B.C.

Fig. 8-2: Nicola Valley Coal & Coke -courtesy of NVAA.

Fig. 8-3: Removing coal from mine. -courtesy of the British Columbia Archives and Records Service. #HP90769.

By June 1906, the track was laid to Coutlee. But there was a shortage of men and materials. More men were brought up from Vancouver to the railway construction camps.

Later that same year the track was laid to Nicola, but lack of railway ties meant only the Coutlee-Spences Bridge section could be used. Construction to Nicola was completed in April, 1907.

While the railway was being built, the mining companies prepared for production. The first carload of Nicola Valley coal left the mines in January, 1907, but it wasn't until June 5, 1907 that the first train load of coal was shipped.

Fig. 8-4: Forksdale: Lots for Sale.
-from the Nicola Herald, March, 1906

Discovery of the coal reserves resulted in immediate expansion of business interests in the valley. A company town named Middlesboro was built at the mouth of Coal Gully. Building lots measuring 50 ft x 120 ft were advertized as being in the centre of the coal belt were sold for as low as $50.00.

The discovery of new coal seams resulted in increased production from 60 to 500 tons a day. Diamondvale Coal and Iron Mines bought the William Charters Ranch that adjoined its production seams and, along with B.C. Amalgamated Coal Company, secured options on other properties owned by Wm. Voght, H. Cleasby and James Chapman.

Fig. 8-5: The Nicola Valley Coal & Coke Company operation was known as Middlesboro Colliery and the settlement, as Middlesboro. -Hooper photograph courtesy of May Chapman.

Fig. 8-6:
Letterhead.
-courtesy of
NVAA

NICOLA VALLEY COAL & COKE COMPANY, LTD.

RAILWAY WEIGHTS GOVERN
ALL SHIPMENTS.

HEAD OFFICE:
VANCOUVER, B.C.

RAILWAY STATION:
COUTLEE, B.C.

COLLIERIES,
MIDDLESBORO, B.C.,   *March 8th 1909*

The Dinky Engine (smaller and narrower than a regular train engine) was used to haul coal from Nicola Valley Coal & Coke Co.'s No. 2 Mine to their main tipple. The track passed to the south, just behind the Middlesboro houses.

Fig. 8-7: The Dinky Engine. John Leese, ?, Teddy Pierce, Dave Brown, Bob Conper, ?, ?, and Blondy Hodgson.
-courtesy of NVAA.

Page 51

Even though problems occurred there were continued advancements in the coal industry and mining communities. By 1909 a union was organized. Merritt was growing with construction of a hotel, hospital, office building, bank and school.

A typical work day was ten hours with average wages of $4.00 a day. Coal mining was not an easy job. Hand tools were used and air circulation was poor. When exposed to air, shale rock decomposes making it necessary to frequently replace timber in tunnels. Minor cave-ins were common. Maintenance costs were high and with the formation of the union, strikes began for higher wages and better working conditions.

Fig. 8-8: Mr. Kinny (far left) outside Aberdeen Mine. -courtesy of NVAA.

Fig. 8-9: George Hallinan. A rope riders job was to take empty coal cars down into the mine (The Prospect), and return with full ones. Circa 1930. -courtesy of the British Columbia Archives and Records Service. #HP90768.

Fig. 8-11: Below: Early type of miners hat and a bird cage. Canaries were used to warn miners of high gas levels. -courtesy of the Canadian Museum of Civilization. #77-6396.

Fig. 8-10: An explosion, on March 7, 1912 caused by damp gas igniting coal dust took the lives of seven men and seriously injured three in the mining tragedy at Diamondvale Mine. -courtesy of NVAA.

Coal shipments were continuous until 1924. Exhausted coal seams in some mines and decreased production in others affected the industry. The depression of the 1930s set in and coal mining declined rapidly. The final blow came when the railways converted to deisel-electric power in the 1950s. Only a fraction of coal reserves were recovered during the five decades of mining.

There was interest in hard rock prospects in the valley as early as 1875, but with the exception of some production on the east side of Stump Lake in the 1880s, at the Aberdeen Mine about 1900 and at OK mine in the Highland Valley, there was little progress in the field until Craigmont Mines went into production in 1961. The original company, Pinecrest Gold Mines, was formed in 1946 and changed its name to Craigmont Mines in 1952.

In July 1958, 20 miners from Salmo arrived to start working on an exploration tunnel. By July 1961, 226 men were employed and land near the C.P.R. track at Coyle, (Lower Nicola), had been purchased to facilitate shipping. Buttons were pushed in September 1961, setting huge grinding mills into operation and Craigmont began production of copper concentrate. A year later it had 404 employees.

Fig. 8-12: Neil McDiarmid, Founder and Director of Craigmont Mines Ltd. -courtesy of Craigmont Mines.

Fig. 8-13: Ken Kiernan, Minister of Mines, officially starts Craigmont operation September 15, 1961. Standing next to him are G. Gordon & J. Simpson. -courtesy of Craigmont Mines.

Japanese contracts, which gave the company its initial thrust, ended in 1975 and the mine became dependant on North American markets. The 22 years that Craigmont mine functioned were successful despite fluctuating copper prices and often adverse mining conditions.

In 1978, a decrease in copper prices forced a staff reduction to 300 men. Another decrease in 1981 reduced the number of employees to 204. By 1981, copper ore reserves were running out and work crews prepared to close and seal the portals. Mill conversion was made to process the balance of the coarse iron ore stockpile, a byproduct of the mining operation.

Fig. 8-15: Electric locomotive hauling out copper ore. -courtesy of Craigmont Mines.

Fig. 8-14: Craigmont pit near completion of open-pit mining in 1967. -courtesy of Craigmont Mines.

Exploration continued until April 1982 in hopes of finding another economic ore body, but the search was unsuccessful.

In December 1982, the flip of a switch ended mill operations at Craigmont and work began to return to nature the land where nearly 38 million tons of ore had been removed.

9: LOGGING

In the early 1870s, small sawmills were in operation in Nicola Valley (Lower Nicola), The Forks (Merritt), Nicola Lake (Upper Nicola) and Quilchena. Lumber produced was for local use. These mills were part of farm operations and did not operate as full time businesses. The Murray Church was built in 1876 of lumber from nearby Mill Creek.

Fig. 9-1: Loggers working in the Coldwater area. Circa 1920. -courtesy of T.B. Meeker.

By the early 1900s, railway construction and development of the coal mines resulted in an increase in logging and milling. The influx of workers and the growth of the business community gave further impetus as new homes and business blocks were constructed. Horse logging was carried on until the introduction of machinery in the 1930s. Many small mills were built near stands of timber and rough lumber was transported to planers in Merritt. Mill sites often included bunkhouses for single men and small homes for families.

Fig. 9-2: Nicola Pine Mills. -courtesy of NVAA.

Fig. 9-3: Nicola Pine Mills after its move to where Tolko Industries is now located in Merritt. -courtesy of NVAA.

A sawmill was established in 1906 at Canford by Andrew McGoran who sold to Henry Meeker in 1910. Shortly afterward the mill was destoyed by fire. Meeker re-located about two miles south at Spius Creek. A spur line was built from the Spences Bridge-Nicola railway to this new location. The community included a sawmill, box factory, planer mill, company store and post office. By 1919, it was the largest sawmill in the interior of the province.

Fig. 9-4: Above: Gus Brolin tackling a Ponderosa Pine (1921). -courtesy of NVAA.

Fig. 9-5: Top Right: Logging railway built up Midday Creek for Nicola Pine Mills Ltd. by Dewolf & Ham, 1920. -courtesy of NVAA.

On May 27, 1919, the Nicola Pine Mills plant and yard at Canford Mills was completely destroyed by fire. Defects in electric wiring in the community hall were deemed responsible for the fire. After negotiations, Meeker re-located to Merritt on property now known as the Tolko Mill. He built a small sawmill in Brookmere to manufacture lumber for construction of the new mill.

Fig. 9-6: Bottom Right: Loading logs using a boom and horse. -courtesy of NVAA

Fig. 9-7: Loading logs at Patchetts for delivery to Merritt.(c.1920) -courtesy of T.B. Meeker.

Fig. 9-8: The Mac's, Herb Hetcher, 1925.

During the depression of the 1930s, Nicola Pine Mills went bankrupt. In 1938, Bill and Harold Pooley started logging with only two horses by first picking up private lumber, then logging for Douglas Lake Cattle Co., A.L. Patchett and Pacific Veneer.

By early the 1940s, logging became more mechanized. Horses and scrapers that were used to build logging roads were replaced by tractors. In 1943, the Long Brothers took over the Nicola Pine Mills property. Pooleys logged for them until 1946.

At the end of the Second World War a new mill was built near the center of Merritt (Aspen Planers) and another on Nicola Pine's site. Small sawmills were slowly phased out when it became more economical to haul logs to larger mills.

Fig. 9-9: J. Potts, Canford, 1929. -photos courtesy of NVAA

Fig. 9-10: Skidding logs to landing. -courtesy of NVAA.

Fig. 9-11: Hauling to mill. -courtesy of NVAA.

Fig. 9-12: Loading. -courtesy of NVAA.

Today there are five major mills in Merritt including Weyerhaeuser, Aspen Planers, Tolko, Ardew Wood Products and NMV Lumber. Modern machines and equipment cut and move logs to landings. From there they are loaded onto trucks to be taken to the sawmills. Mill and logging operations in the Nicola Valley employ several hundred people. Beyond the grazing lands lie large tracts of timber. This is "our logging country."

10: TRANSPORTATION

When white men came to the valley they found a network of native trails that had been in use for thousands of years. The Hudson's Bay Company made use of this network in establishing their trade routes to the Pacific coast. They were followed by the packers taking cattle and supplies to the Cariboo and, later, cattle drives to the lower mainland markets. In the 1870s, wagon roads were constructed through the main valleys followed by railway tracks in the early 1900s.

Fig. 10-1. Blind Charlie's Freighting. Cultus (Blind) Charlie (far left), George Bent and Neil Bent.(c.1900) -from the Dr. Sutton Album.

Nicola Valley, Armstrongs and other stage-coach companies made connections between the valley and Spences Bridge, Kamloops and Princeton. "Stopping houses" between destinations offered stage travellers and freighters the opportunity to take a break and drivers to rest or change horses. In winter the stage sometimes switched from wheels to runners.

Fig. 10-2.
Livery Stables had a large barn and wagon yard for horses and freight delivery. Also offered was rental or sale of horses.
-courtesy of NVAA.

Fig. 10-3: Thynne's Stopping House. Otter Valley Road. Jack & Mrs. Thynne in photograph. (c.1900) -from the Dr. Sutton Album.

Fig. 10-4. Horse & Buggy (c.1905)-courtesy of Oliver Williams.

Fig. 10-5. 40 Drinks - 40 Winks -Harry Priest photograph.

In summer the main transportation methods up to the 1930s was by buggy, cart, or wagon. In winter wheels were often replaced by runners on sleighs or cutters. Early merchants used horse and buggy for deliveries. Commercial travel also included stage-coach and freight wagon. Horseback riding was common year-around.

Fig. 10-7. Norman Woodward hauling supplies to the Coquahalla for the railroad.-courtesy of Jim McCreight .

Fig. 10-6. The stage in front of a stopping house at Nicola Lake. (1899) -from the Dr. Sutton Album

Fig. 10-8: # 1 at Spences Bridge. (c.1900)
-from the Dr. Sutton Album.

Fig. 10-9: Merritt's railway station. (1938) -courtesy of Phil Wilkinson.

Fig. 10-10:
Clearing snow off
tracks. KVR,
Coquihalla Pass
May 16, 1921.
-courtesy of George
Armstrong.

The Canadian Pcific Railway provided a daily passenger service out of Nicola until 1916 when it was then decreased to once a week. In 1923, the passenger service was discontinued. The station agent then moved to Merritt. Until the 1970s, when the tracks were completely removed, the rail line and stock yards were used only when needed.

In 1910-11, a spur line was built connecting Merritt to the Kettle Valley Railway at Brookmere. Completed in 1916, the K.V.R. linked the Kootenays to the Pacific coast through the Coquihalla Pass until a major washout forced its closure in November 1959.

On May 15, 1989 train service to the Nicola Valley ceased as the C.P.R. moved ahead with plans to abandon the system that served Merritt for more than 80 years.

Fig. 10-11. The first hearse. -courtesy of NVAA.

Fig. 10-12. Abandoned sleigh runner. -courtesy of NVAA.

Fig. 10-14. Upgrading of road along Nicola Lake.
-courtesy of Guy Rose.

Fig. 10-13. George
Childs on Clay Bluffs
near Potatoes Illahee.
-from the Dr. Sutton
Album.

Fig. 10-15: A fine selection of early automobile transport. -courtesy of the British Columbia Records and Archives Service. #HP73155.

Fig. 10-16: Automobiles made it easier for people to travel in groups. -courtesy of NVAA.

Fig. 10-17: Dan Munro's wrecker. -courtesy of Larry Smyth.

One of the first automobiles to come into the valley in the early 1900s was owned by G.B. Armstrong. Motor vehicles for pleasure and commercial use gradually replaced horse power. From the early 1920s until 1935, Bill Hunter offered passenger service by car.

Fig. 10-18: Nicola, B.C. -courtesy of NVAA.

Fig. 10-19: The first airplane to land in the Nicola Valley was in June of 1919 on Blair field, now the Tolko Industries sawmill property.
-courtesy of NVAA.

Fig. 10-20: Bert Orchard. Nicola Valley Challenge Cup. —25 Miles— May 24, 1899. -courtesy of NVAA.

Bus service, owned by Dr. J.J. Gillis and Joe Guichon, was first offered residents of the Nicola Valley in 1935. John Bann ran the service for 12 years linking Merritt, Kamloops, Spences Bridge and Princeton. From 1952 onward, many of the roads were surfaced providing easier access throughout the valley.

After many changes, Merritt's airport was established and on Oct. 16, 1982, the extended runway at Saunders' Field officially opened, although Merritt does not yet have scheduled passenger service.

11: HOTELS

Among the first hotels in the Nicola Valley near the turn of the century were the *Quilchena* at Quilchena, *Driard* at Nicola, *Pioneer* at Coutlee (later named the *Coutlee Hotel*), and Woodward's and Woods' hotels at Lower Nicola.

Fig. 11-1: Driard Hotel, (c.1899). -from the Dr. Sutton Album.

It was recorded in the Nicola Herald April 6, 1908 that, "Mr. Kirby's licence at Quilchena has been transferred to Joseph Guichon, who is running the old place at present." Joseph Guichon built a new Quilchena Hotel at this location and opened it on July 3, 1908. The hotel was initially managed by the son of Mr. and Mrs Guichon, Joseph A. It was expected that Canadian Pacific Railway was going to run past the hotel on the way from Nicola Valley to Kamloops. The railway never did pass, but for the next 10 years the hotel was the focal point of the community. Then for 40 years it remained idle, though not empty.

Before re-opening the Quilchena in the mid 1950s, Guy Rose renovated it, keeping most of the original furnishings and decor. This magnificent hotel, famous for its "old west" grandeur and hospitality, still remains in business today.

Fig. 11-2: Menu from the official opening of the second Quilchena Hotel -taken from the Nicola Herald, July 30, 1908

QUILCHENA HOTEL
LAKE VIEW, QUILCHENA, B.C.
—
Menu, Sunday, August 2nd, 1908
Dinner 1:00 P.M.
—
Russian Caviar
SOUP
Murgutroyd
FISH
Baked Salmon and Egg Sauce
ENTREES
Boiled Fowl and White Sauce
Boiled York Ham
JOINTS
Roast Sirloin of Beef, Yorkshire Pudding
Boiled Ribs of Beef
VEGETABLES
New Potatoes
Kidney Beans   Green Peas
SALAD
Dressed Spring Salad
SWEETS
Tapioca Pudding   Vanilla Custard
Wine Jelly
TEA   M'LAREN'S CHEESE   COFFEE

Fig. 11-3: The first Quilchena Hotel.(c.1900) -from the Dr. Sutton Album.

Fig. 11-4: The 1908 Quilchena Hotel. -courtesy of NVAA.

Page 71

The Hotel Merritt, built on Nicola Avenue in 1906, was the first hotel to operate in Merritt.

Fig. 11-5: Hotel Merritt (1907). -courtesy of the British Columbia Records and Archives Service #A-866.

In 1907, the first Coldwater Hotel was built in Merritt by Wm. McIntyre. Two years later, in 1909, a new Coldwater Hotel was built on the opposite side of the street; the northwest corner of Voght Street and Quilchena Avenue. It became a landmark of the city and still stands today.

Fig. 11-6: Coldwater Hotel during construction (c.1909). -courtesy of the British Columbia Records and Archives Service #HP1840.

Fig. 11-8: Coldwater Hotel (1989). -courtesy of NVAA.

Accommodation High Class

Sixty Large Modern Rooms

COLDWATER HOTEL

The Coldwater is in the centre of things. The Coldwater's guests have every comfort; rooms with baths attached restful beds, absolute security.

Cafe in Connection.

Wm. McIntyre - - - - Proprietor

Fig. 11-7: Coldwater Hotel Advertisement. (c.1910) -courtesy of the Merritt Herald.

Fig. 11-9: "The Adelphi" (c.1915). -courtesy of Gladys Moffat

Two other hotels, built in 1911, and still in operation today are the Adelphi and the Grand. The Adelphi was built as the City Hotel by Andrew and Christine Hoggan. New owners in 1913 changed the name to Adelphi. The Grand Hotel, also built by Andrew Hoggan, first served as a rooming house and was later expanded to a hotel.

The Valnicola and Grasslands hotels opened respectively in November and December, 1961. Fire destroyed both hotels in the 1970s and both were rebuilt on their same location. The Grasslands Hotel has expanded several times to accommodate the needs of the community.

Fig. 11-10: Adelphi (1961).-courtesy of NVAA

Fig. 11-11: Adelphi Advertisement (c.1911) -courtesy of the Merritt Herald.

The City Hotel

This fine new hostelry being completed we are prepared to tickle the palate of the most fastidious; we also carry a splendid line of choice wines, liquors, cigars, and cigarettes.

Andrew Hoggan, - - Prop.

Fig. 11-12: Left to Right: John Hoggan, ?, Alexander Hoggan (Proprietor), Jock Dennison, Christina Hoggan (Proprietress), ?, and ? in front of the original Grand Hotel. - courtesy of Jim Hoggan

Fig. 11-13: The "new" Grand Hotel. -courtesy of the British Columbia Records and Archives Service #HP84452.

Fig. 11-14: The original Grand Hotel bar. A fire destroyed the hotel and a new one was built. -courtesy of Jim Hoggan.

GRAND HOTEL

The only tiled bar in the valley.

GOOD BOARD AND CLEAN ROOMS

FIRST CLASS LIQUORS AND CIGARS

Our Aim: Corteous treatment to all.

Mrs. Christina Hoggan, Proprietress

Nicola Avenue, Merritt.

Fig. 11-15: Grand Hotel Advertisement (Undated.) -courtesy of the Merritt Herald.

12: SCHOOLS

The first Nicola Valley school district was created July 1874. Trustees were William Charters, John Chapman and Harvey H. Woodward.

Fig. 12-1: Nicola School. -courtesy of NVAA

From $750.00 raised, two school-houses were built. One was near the junction of Nicola and Coldwater Rivers, known as 'east' school and the other about a mile west of Ten-Mile Creek, known as 'west' school or Woodward Settlement. School commenced by the summer of 1875 with about twenty-two pupils and Archie Irwin as the first teacher. For the first few months he taught alternately for half a day in each school and after the first year, school was carried on in the two schools on alternate days.

In these early years the community provided school facilities while the government paid teachers salaries.

Fig. 12-2: Grade Six Robin Hood Play. -courtesy of Mary Moyes.

Fig. 12-3:

Lower Nicola School Class 1906

Back Row: Mary Dodding, Perry Johnston, Jack Chapman, Fred Woodward.
Second Row: Celia Garcia, David Dodding, Bella McKitrick, Alma Coutlee, Jennie Woodward, Bertha Woodward.
Front Row: Dorothy Lindley, Alfred Smith, David Lindley, Chrissie Woodward, Willie Dodding, John Dodding, Olive Smith.
Teacher: Miss Mooney
-from the Dr. Sutton Album.

Nicola Lake School was established in early 1883 with trustees Peter Fraser, William Palmer and Robert Scott. After the second year, attendance fell and the school was closed permanently.

In 1907, government schools were established at Aspen Grove and Coldwater. Mammette Lake School opened in 1906 or 1907.

Fig. 12-4:

Back Row: **Canford Public School** (1923)
Berta Fraser, Margaret Richardson, Marion Lindbergh, Clayton Lindbergh, Walter James, & Ralph James.

Front Row: Margorie Cummings, Delnor Lindbergh, Jack Fraser, Eddie Richardson, Avard Lindbergh, Jimmy Cummings, John Richardson, & John Siderfin
-courtesy of NVAA

Fig. 12-5: Lower Nicola School. -courtesy of Clara Larson

Fig. 12-6:
Right:
Back Row: **Mammette Lake School** (Early 50's)
Lottie McDougall, Joanne Hunter, Myrna Petrie, Larry Steffens, Pat Steffens, & Allan Steffens

Front Row: Allan Hunter, Karen Watson, Arlene Atkinson, Ted Crabtree, & Gary Davis (with bat).Squatting isCarl Watson, Jerry McDougall & Scott Atkinson
-courtesy of Pat Brkich.

In 1908, Merritt School District was formed from parts of the Lower Nicola and Nicola districts. During 1908-09 school was held in Hyland Hall in Merritt. Mrs. Priest, the first teacher, had thirteen students in her class. By April 1909, Ernest Fraser replaced Mrs. Priest. The class had increased to 60 and construction of a two-room school house had been approved.

Fig. 12-7:
Above: **First Merritt School Class of 1908**
Back Row: Annie King, Tena Voght, Edith Page, Mable Nash, Mona King, & Lena Voght & Mrs. H. Priest
Front Row: Jenny Wade, William Page, Johnny Thibideau, Nelson Brolin, Johnny MacDonald, & Eric Brolin
-courtesy of NVAA

In August 1909, H.S. Cleasby, J.A. Menzies and H.E. Forsythe were elected by acclamation to the first Merritt school board.

The first principal for Merritt's senior high and elementary schools, Leo Edward Morrissey, held this position from 1913 until his retirement in 1956.

In 1946, the new Merritt School District was created to take in most of the outlying areas from Aspen Grove to the upper end of Stump Lake and from Dot to the northeast reaches of the Douglas Lake Ranch.

Fig. 12-8: Mrs. H. Priest. (1910). School was first held in this tent.
-courtesy of the British Columbia Records and Archives Service #HP90709.

Fig. 12-9: **Aspen Grove School (1953)**
Carol Nicklin, Joyce McLeod, Betty Nicklin, Mrs Grandbois, Russell Grandbois, Monica McLeod, Marion ?, Grace Nicklin, Pat Garcia, Allan Keehne, Rodney Keehne, George Garcia Jr., Kenny ?, Lee McLeod & Gary Grandbois
-courtesy of Monica McLeod

Fig. 12-10: **Mr. Morrissey's First High School Class in Merritt.** Left to right: Elin Gavelin, Ena Ransom, Connie Batten, Olive Smith -courtesy of Jim McCreight

Fig. 12-11: **Merritt Graduation Class of 1952.**
Left to Right: Doreen Tarzwell, Myrtle Shuttleworth, Bruce Josephson, Mable Lawrence, Doreen Hunter, Donna Cassidy
-courtesy of NVAA

Today the Merritt School District includes five elementary and two high schools and the alternate school with an enrollment of 1,185. Other schools in the area include the Maranatha Christian, Nicola Valley Christian, Coldwater Native, Shulus Native schools.

Cariboo College offers extension programs in Merritt and the new Nicola Valley Institute of Technology is opeating from buildings in Merritt and Nicola.

Schoolhouses in early years were also occasionally used for religious services and local meetings. Today they are restricted mainly to school events.

Fig. 12-13:

Graduating Class of 1959

Back Row:	Gerry Gardner, Larry Ovington, Albert Brisson
Second Row:	Pat Steffens, Sharon Bland, Donna Moyes
Third Row:	Arthur Benzer, Catherine Batten, Fred Sterling
Front Row:	Elaine Smith, Joan Nisbet

-courtesy of Ken Moyes

Fig. 12-12:

Merritt Secondary School Staff of 1959

Back Row:	Robert Taylor, ? , Bob Turnbull, & Mr. Farr
Middle Row:	Barbara Langley (secretary), Leo Morrissey, Gertrude Reid, & Mrs. Saunders.
Front Row:	? (secretary), Mr. Boulanger, Mrs. Farr & Helen Nisbet. -courtesy of NVAA.

13: PUBLIC SERVICES

Around 1870, moves were taken to establish a postal service in the Nicola Valley. The first post office opened on August 1, 1872 at the Nicola Lake home of John Clapperton.

Fig. 13-1: The First Post Office in the Nicola Valley. Harry Priest photograph. -courtesy of the British Columbia Records and Archives Service.

Fig. 13-2: Nicola Valley General Hospital. Harry Priest photograph. -courtesy of the British Columbia Records and Archives Service. #HP90755

Fig. 13-3: **Merritt Graduate Nurses**
Back Row: Greta Ewart, Olive Smith, Inez Dunlop, Miss Vicar, Dorothy Pooley.
Front Row: Jean Fairley, Phylis Blanchet, Inga Teit, Selma Smith.
-courtesy of Inga Perkin (Teit).

Fig. 13-4: **Graduate Nurses of 1919.** Gladys Batten (left), and Mary Bond. (below) -Harry Priest photograph.

Doctors in the valley during the late 1800s included Thomas W. Lambert, A.W. Pearse, J.D. McGuire, John Chipp, M.M. Murphy and Alfred Martin Sutton.

In 1902, Dr. George Tutill purchased Dr. Sutton's practice at Nicola and was also appointed resident physician by the government.

During construction of the rail lines, small hospitals were established to serve rail construction employees. Dr. Tutill was in charge of service from 22 Mile to Nicola and Dr. Cyrill S. Williams was in charge from Spences Bridge to 10 Mile. Upon completion of the railway, Williams moved to Merritt and Tutill remodelled the construction hospital for his practice. Dr. J.J. Gillis joined Dr. Williams in 1911.

Nicola Valley General Hospital was built on Priest Avenue and was officially opened April 20, 1912. The Superintendent was Dr. Williams and practitioners were Dr. Gillis and Dr. Tutill. A nursing school operated with two years of practical training in Merritt followed by a third year in Vancouver.

Dr. Gillis officially opened the present Nicola Valley General Hospital on March 21, 1964.

In earlier years, public services were often house visits by the missionary priest, minister or local doctor. Father Le Jeune held mass and performed many baptisms and weddings in family homes.

In 1909, the police moved from Nicola to Merritt.

To serve his patients, Dr. Gillis's methods of travel included horseback, commandeering a special locomotive and even borrowing a sectionman's handcar.

Fig. 13-5: Percy Carr. (C. 1930) -courtesy of NVAA.

Fig. 13-6: Dr. J.J. Gillis.(c.1911) -courtesy of E. Bristow.

The first church in the Nicola Valley was built at Nicola in 1876. It was later named the Murray Church in honour of its founder, Reverand George Murray. Edwin Dalley donated ground in 1899 for St. John the Baptist Anglican Church in Nicola. Both Nicola churches have been restored.

The Methodist Church, completed in 1909, was the first church built in Merritt. It now serves as a funeral chapel. In 1908, William Voght secured ground for the Presbyterian Church which was completed by 1910. His was the first funeral service to be held in the new church. Merritt's first Anglican parish, formed in 1908, initially held services in Hyland Hall. The church, completed in 1913, was built through volunteer assistance, pledges and a mortgage through J.B. Greaves, the founder of the Douglas Lake Cattle Company. The Catholic Sacred Heart Church, built on land donated by Jesus Garcia, was completed in

Fig. 13-7: Murray Church at Nicola. -courtesy of Murphy Shewchuk.

1911. In 1927, the Methodist and Presbyterian churches in the valley amalgamated to become the Trinity United Church.

Fig. 13-8: Sacred Heart Church. -courtesy of NVAA.

Mission churches were built at Douglas Lake, Quilchena, Coldwater and Shulus. In 1887, Father Le Jeune was involved in the construction of St. Nicholas' Church at Douglas Lake. In 1893, with the help of Joseph Guichon, he built the original Our Lady of Lourdes Church at Quilchena.

St. Paul's Church at Coldwater, built in 1901, was named to honour the Saint and also to give recognition to its main builder, Paul Satchie. The earliest record of services held at All Saint's Anglican at Shulus was in 1904. The church of Immaculate Conception at Shulus was dedicated in June, 1905.

Fig. 13-9: Flower Cottage. -courtesy of NVAA.

Fig. 13-10: Merritt Funeral Chapel. -courtesy of NVAA.

The first Court House was built on Coutlee Avenue and is the Flower Cottage today. The construction of the present courthouse was completed in 1914. The location changed when Mayor Archie Jackson took the Coutlee Avenue location in exchange for his lot on Nicola Avenue.

N.J. Barwick, Merritt's first undertaker, moved from Nicola. Horses rented from Dan Munro's livery pulled the hearse until horses were no longer used. In 1926, that same hearse was fitted onto the chassis of a one-ton truck. In 1927, the Methodist Church became the funeral chapel. John Bann became the funeral director in 1945 and remained until his retirement in 1987.

The Merritt Volunteer Fire Brigade was initiated in 1911 on Merritt's incorporation day. The fire fighting equipment, a 30 gallon water/chemical cart, was pulled by hand unless a passing horse or motor vehicle could be commandeered. The first fire truck was purchased in 1927 and the first fire hall was located on the corner of Granite Avenue and Garcia Street.

In 1897, A.E. Howse introduced telephone service to the Nicola Valley. November, 1928 marked the inauguration of a direct telephone link between Merritt and Vancouver.

Fig. 13-11: Ladder wagon and hose reel. The two men standing on the wagon are; Leo Morrissey and Nat Barwick (fire chief), seated are; ?, Jack Riley, Bill Riley, George Riley, Billy McGinnis, ?, ?. Standing in front is Constable Offley, ?, & ?. (c.1925). -courtesy of Maude Riley.

14: WARS

Fig. 14-1: **Second World War Forestry Corps**
Back Row: Frank Dunnigan, Bernard Dunnigan, Archie Allan, Gordon Cameron, Tom Rodgers, Matt Ovington, Bill Dobbie
Middle Row: Bob Hooper, Ray Fairley, Ernie Gavelin, Jim Kinnear, Capt. Ted Martin, Jack Greenwood, Hugh Campbell, Bob Walker, Lloyd
              Beckman
Front Row: Kelly Clark, Tom Sanderson, Jim Maxwell, Paddy Kearns, Bob Fairfoull, Derry Ewart.   -courtesy of Jimmy Maxwell.

The war effort in the Nicola Valley took on many forms.

During the First World War, Chief Johnny Chilihitsa, famous for his thoroughbred race horses, raised light horses for the cavalry and artillery.

High quality spruce lumber produced in the valley was used for aeroplane manufacture.

Healing from the pains of war, was and is, as individual as the memories that people choose to share.

Fig. 14-2: Chief John Chilihitsa. -courtesy of the Canadian Museum of Civilization, National Museums of Canada #18416

Fig. 14-3: **First World War Forestry Corps.** (1914) -courtesy of Jim McCreight.

Fig. 14-4: **Lower Nicola Home Guards**
Back Row: Fred Dodding, Frank Nelson, Bart Dodding, Wilfred Blundell, Homer Schover, ? Bergain, Ken Long, Joe Whitaker, & ? Gavelin
Middle Row: Ed Kinvig, Tom Hanna, Jack Sparks, Joe Schindler, Bob Whitaker, Felex Allison, & Tom Bevan
Front Row: Reese Bevan, Dick Hanna, Jeff Hardiman, Fred Woodward, Ed Neale, Ron Bevan, & John Dodding
(c.1943)
-courtesy of Jim McCreight.

Fig. 14-5: **Red Cross Workers**
Starting at top left: Mrs. Archie Hardy, Margaret Carr, ?, Celia Barrett, Mrs. Tommy Williams, ?, Harriet Dodding, Florence Jobling, ?, Mrs. Belshaw, Mrs. Sowerby, Olive McCreight, ?, Mrs. Josephson, ?, ?, ?, Mrs. Fred Gay, Edith Ingleby, ?, Mrs. Pete Moyes, Mrs. Harry Collett, Ellen Bamber, Mrs. Charlie Collett, Ellen Gerrard, Zella Mayon, Mrs. George Beveridge, ?, Della Clemens, & Mrs. Percy Boyd
-courtesy of NVAA.

Fig. 14-6:   **Merritt Cenotaph**

Boer War (1899-1902)
First World War (1914-1918)
Korean War (1950-1953)

D. Hogg	J.F. Nash	W. Dryborough
P. Hynd	H. Nicol	W. Tommage
J. Service	W. Murray	J. Bauch
J. Connor	R. Davidson	J.C. McGee
E.W. Jones	W. Baxter	W. Lindsay
J. Paterson	J. Birch	T.H. Beans
J. Scobie	A. Bone	A. Shuttleworth
H.C. Fisher	G. Mitchell	R. McCoid
S. Poole	R. Cochenour	H.P. Wright
J. McNaulty	A.J. Hogg	T. Tilamoose
J.L. Busk	A.J. Berkely	G. Collins
R. Ferguson	J.A. Hobson	B. Barnes
L. Cook	W.L. Bradley	J. Harrower
J. Paul	J. Wilcox	F. King
R.C. Singleton		
W.P. Thompson		

Second World War (1939-1945)

B.H. Barber	E.L. Barrett	W.J. Dunnigan
J.A. Dalton	W.J. Koller	G.S. Christianson
L.F. Fairley	J.T. Hardy	A. Hogg
W.A. Houston	D.P. McIvor	A.F. McDougal
W.A. McIvor	M. Ovington	H. Purvis
E. Sowerby	E. Walker	L.F. Boulanger

-courtesy of NVAA.

15: SPORTS

Fig. 15-1:   **Merritt High School Baseball Team: (c.1926)**
Back Row: M. Barwick, J. Dalton, S. Phillips, R. Jones, A. Collett and L.E. Morrissey.
Front Row: L. Meeker, J. Nisbet, M. Dalton, & J. Cassidy and N. Brewster.
            -courtesy of the British Columbia Archives and Records Service #HP90757.

Fig. 15-2:
Merritt High School Basketball Team
(1932 Winners of the CPR Cup)

Left to Right: Rosmond Riley, Della Clemens, Peggy Hallinan, Jean Corkle, Viola Wade, Joan Mills and Isabell Geater.
-courtesy of NVAA.

Fig. 15-3:   **1924 Robinson Cup Winners**

Back Row: Walter Dallas, Tom Dobbie, Joe Haddad and Archie Samuel.
Third Row: Dick Clark, Bill Fairley, Frank Hill, Bob Cooper and Charles Isitt.
Second Row: Bill Hallinan, David Greaves, George Isitt and John Dunningan.
Front Row: Alex Thompson, David Fairley, Frank McStay and John Ovington.
                -courtesy of George Isitt.

Fig. 15-4:   **Coy Cup Winners, 1936**

Back Row: E. Martin (coach), Noah Boyden,
             A. "Scotty" Collins, Jim Brown,
             Tom Petrie (pres.), Jim Nisbet
             and Bill Cassidy.
Front Row: Jim Neilson, Allan Collett,
             George Hallinan, Victor Martin
             (mascot), Alex Stelmock,
             Jim Hogan and Johnny Cassidy.
             -courtesy of NVAA.

Fig. 15-5: Lacrosse Team in late 1890's.
Only one name is available. In front at far left is
J.N. Moore.
-courtesy of NVAA.

Fig. 15-6: **Curling** (undated) Left to Right: Harry Priest, Bill Cranna, Jim Ellis and Bill Innes -courtesy of NVAA.

Fig. 15-7: **1913 Nicola Polo Team** -courtesy of NVAA.

Polo was a major sport in the valley. In 1896, a club was formed at Nicola and by 1906, joined with clubs from Quilchena and Kamloops. World wars, club disorganization and the lack of players caused the folding of the Nicola Polo Club.

Fig. 15-8: **Baseball**

Back Row: George Beatty, Bill Cassidy, Archie Hardy, Howard Ransom, Allan Collett and Harold Cartwright

Front Row: ?, Kelly Clark, Jim Neilson, Johnny Cassidy and Frank McStay.

-courtesy of Archie Hardy.

16: HUNTING & FISHING

Fig. 16-1: Harold Greig. (undated) -courtesy of NVAA.

Fig. 16-2: Sigurd Teit and Henry Cross display their catch of mule deer. Taken in 1950 at Summer Range (Logan Lake area). -courtesy of Sigurd Teit.

Fig. 16-3: Fish caught at Boot Lake. Jack Isitt, Steve Oldham and George Isitt. -courtesy of George Isitt.

Fig. 16-4: "Youthful Sports" Postcard. Children fishing in the Coldwater River. (c.1909) -Harry Priest photograph.

17: ENTERTAINMENT

Fig. 17-1: Central Hall. -courtesy of NVAA.

Fig. 17-1: Central Hall. -courtesy of NVAA.

The Annual Bachelors Ball was a gala event with personal invitations sent out to single ladies of the valley with the hopeful prospects of meeting that "special" one. ·

Victoria Day included horse racing, gymkhana events, athletic sports and a parade. Special train fares were offered when the celebrations were held at Lower Nicola. The early stampedes were an event which most people in the valley looked forward to and prepared for months in advance. The parades, with marching bands and floats, were grand affairs.

Fig. 17-2: Cowboy Race. Nicola, July 1st, 1910.

Fig. 17-3: Hurdle Race. Nicola, July 1st, 1910.   Harry Priest photographs.

Fig. 17-4: Ladies Race. Nicola, July 1st, 1910.

Page 99

Fig. 17-5: Diamond Jubilee.
July 1st, 1927.
-Harry Priest photograph.

Fig. 17-6: Merritt Stampede, 1935. -courtesy of NVAA.

Fig. 17-7: Merritt Stampede, 1940. -courtesy of NVAA.

Fig. 17-8:   **First May Day Celebration. (1915)**
Left to Right: Glennie Langstaff, Ruth Wade (attendants), Fred Grimmett (page), Myrtle Kennedy (May Queen), Dorothy Langstaff (page),
Dorothy Ransom and Winnifred Boothroyd (attendants). -courtesy of NVAA.

Fig. 17-9: **Sunshine Orchestra (c.1939.)**
Left to Right: Tom Cook, J. Grant, J. Smith, S. Gerrard, J. Fairley and J. Miller -courtesy of NVAA.

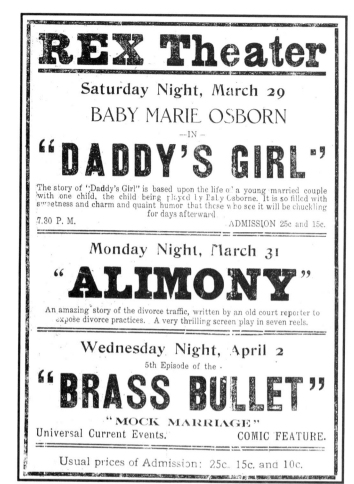

Fig. 17-10: Rex Theater Advertisement
-from the Nicola Herald (undated.)

Fig. 17-11: **Pageant** (c.1918)
Back Row: Bobbie Hogg, Bella Cassidy & Donald Hogg
Front Row: Johnny Dunlop, ? Dunlop, ? Bresnick, ? Ryan, Bill Fairley, Jean Scott, Allan Collett, ? , & Mary Barnes
-courtesy of Margaret (Crawford) Walker.

LOWER NICOLA PICNIC:

Mrs. Marcus Woodward, Fred Woodward, Bob Johnson, Olive Smith, George Murray, Mrs. Richard, Mrs. Dodding Sr., Jack Chapman, Mrs. Mickle, Willie Dodding, Ed Cousins, Mr. Fraser, Johnnie Dodding, Norman Woodward, Mrs. Tutill, Mrs. Bob Johnson, Grace Woodward, Mrs. Riley, Flo Hunter, Dr. Tutill, Mrs. A. Carrington, Sid Soloman, Arthur Carrington, Mrs.

Fig. 17-12: **Lower Nicola Picnic.** (Circa 1904.)
-photo courtesy of NVAA, names courtesy of the Merritt Herald.

David Dodding, Mr. Gilderdale, Mrs. Pie, Alfred Smith, Fred Riley, Menetta Pie, Gordon Winnie, Jim Woodward, Rev. Pie, Fred McInnis, Henry Woodward, Pauline Steffens, Jimmie Smith, Mary Dodding, Nat Steward, Bertha Woodward, Mrs. Steward, Mr. Richard, Laurie Carrington, Marion Woodward, Mrs. Bradbent, Mrs. Nat Barwick, Mrs. Dan McInnis, Dorothy Car-

Jim Chapman, Harvey Woodward, Mrs. Harry Cleasby, Birdie Starrett, W. Riley, Mr. McGregor, Eleanor Starrett, Bell McKitrick, Harry Winnie, Mildred McInnis, (?), H. Winnie's son, Josie McKitrick, Jennie Woodward, Gertie Carrington, Conston Smith, Chrisie Woodward, Mr. Starrett, Mrs. Jim Smith, rington, Mrs. Lettice, Bobby Carrington, Henry Lindley, Mr. Barwick, Lyle Hardiman, Myrtle Woodward, Bart Dodding, Pearl McInnis, Clarence Woodward, Billy Snider, Perry Johnson, Marcus Woodward, Bob Dodding, Boy, Frank Woodward, Ramona Woodward, Mr. Dodding Sr.

18: THEN & NOW

Fig. 18-1: The southwest corner of Quilchena Avenue and Voght Street. (Across from the Coldwater Hotel) (c.1912). -courtesy of NVAA.

Fig. 18-2: Southwest corner of Quilchena and Voght.(1989). -courtesy of Sigurd Teit.

Fig. 18-3: Quilchena Avenue, looking west from Garcia Street (c.1920).
-Harry Priest photograph.

QUILCHENA AVENUE MERRITT B.C.   PHOTO BY H. PRIEST

Fig. 18-4: Quilchena Avenue, looking west from Garcia Street (1989).
-courtesy of Sigurd Teit.

BIBLIOGRAPHY

Bailey, Frank; *Nicola Similkameen and Tulameen Valleys*; Ward Ellwood & Pound, Printers, Vancouver; (c.1912).

British Columbia Cattlemen's Assoc.; *Landmarks and Branding Irons.*

Cleasby, Henry S.; *The Nicola Valley In Review*; Merritt Herald Ltd., Merritt; 1958.

Cliftendon, Newton H.; *Guide Through British Columbia.*

Dawe, Alan; *Profile of a Nation*; MacMillan Company of Canada Ltd., Toronto; 1969.

Dolby, Elizabeth; *Fur Trade and Culture Change Among the Okanagan Indians*;

Duff, Wilson; *The Indian History of British Columbia*; Department of Recreation & Conservation, Victoria; 1964.

Fox, Tammy & Lean, Pat; *Merritt Her History and Symbols of Identity*; Merritt Herald, Merritt; 1985.

Geographic Board-Canada; *Handbook of Indians of Canada*; Coles Publishing Co., Toronto; 1971, 1974.

Morse, J.J.; *Indians of Interior British Columbia.*

Shewchuk, Murphy; *Exploring the Nicola Valley*; Douglas & McIntyre Ltd, Vancouver; 1981.

Shewchuk, Murphy; *The Craigmont Story*; Hancock House Publisher Ltd., Surrey; 1983.

Steffens, Sophia; *The Land of Chief Nicola.*

Surtees, Ursala; *Lak-La Hai-ee*; Lamont-Surtees, Kelowna; 1974.

Teit, James; *The Thompson Indians of British Columbia*; AMS Press Inc., New York; 1975.

Veillette, John & White, Gary; *Early Indian Village Churches*; University of British Columbia Press, Vancouver; 1977.

Woolliams, Nina G.; *Cattle Ranch*; Douglas & McIntyre, Vancouver; 1979.

NEWSPAPERS AND PERIODICALS

Fraser, Berta; "Early Logging in the Nicola Valley"; *Nicola Valley Historical Quarterly*; (July, 1979), Vol. 2-No. 3.

Lean, Pat & Howes, Katharine; "Commemorating: William Henry Voght, 'The Father of Merritt'"; *Nicola Valley Historical Quarterly*; (April, 1979), Vol. 2-No. 2.

Lean, Pat; "Profiles"; *Nicola Valley Historical Quarterly*; (April, 1979), Vol. 2-No. 2.

Lean, Pat; "Ranchers"; *Nicola Valley Historical Quarterly*; (Dec., 1981), Vol. 4-Nos. 3 & 4.

Lean, Pat; "The Town at the Foot of the Lake"; *Nicola Valley Historical Quarterly*; (April, 1981), Vol. 4-No. 2.

"Post Offices-Nicola Valley"; *Nicola Valley Historical Quarterly*; (October, 1979), Vol. 2-No. 4.

Shewchuk, Murphy; "The Brigade Trails"; *Nicola Valley Historical Quarterly*; (October, 1980) Vol. 3-No. 4.

The Merritt Herald.

The Nicola Herald.

The Vancouver Sun.

Veale, Jack R.; "The Coquihalla Route"; *Nicola Valley Historical Quarterly*; (January, 1982) Vol. 5-No.1.

INDEX

(An asterisk indicates an illustration.)

10-Mile, 83
14-Mile, 22
21-Mile Ranch, 31
22-Mile House, 31
22-Mile, 83

A

Aberdeen Camp, 48*
Aberdeen Mine, 52*, 54
Adelphi Hotel, 74*
All Saint's Anglican Church (Shulus), 85
Allan, Archie, 89*
Allison, Felex, 90*
Alternate School, 81
Anderson's Trail, 12
Anderson, Alexander Caulfield, 12*
Archer, Frank, 44*
Ardew Wood Products, 61,
Armstrong's Departmental Store, 33*
Armstrong, George B., 24, 25*, 31, 33, 68
Armstrongs (stage-coach company), 63
Aspen Grove Road House, 29*
Aspen Grove School, 78, 80*
Aspen Grove Store, 29*
Aspen Grove, 12, 29, 42, 44*, 84*
Aspen Planers, 61
Athapaskan, 1
Atkinson, Arlene, 78*
Atkinson, Scott, 78*
Axten Fox Ranch, 47*
Axten, A.E., 47

B

B.C. Amalgamated Coal Co., 50
B.C. Beef Market, 105*

Bachelor's Ball, 98
Bamber, Ellen, 90*
Bank of Montreal, 33, 37*
Bann, John, 69, 86
Barber, B.H., 91*
Barnes, B., 91*
Barnes, Mary, 102*
Barrett, Celia, 90*
Barrett, E.L., 91*
Barrett, Lloyd, 41*
Barwick & Co., 28*
Barwick, M., 92*
Barwick, Mrs. Nat, 103*
Barwick, Nat J., 86, 87*, 103*
Baseball, 95*
Basketry, 8*
Batten, Catherine, 81*
Batten, Connie, 80*
Batten, Gladys, 83*
Battersby, Mr., 37*
Bauch, J., 91*
Baxter, W., 91*
Beak, Charles H., 39
Beans, T.H., 91*
Beatty, George, 95*
Beaver Ranch, 22, 39
Beckerman, Lloyd, 88*
Belshaw, Mrs., 90*
Bent, George, 24, 25*, 62*
Bent, Neil, 62*
Benzer, Arthur, 81*
Bergain, ? , 90*
Berkley, A.J., 91*
Bevan, Reese, 90*
Bevan, Ron, 90*
Bevan, Tom, 90*
Beveridge, Mrs. George, 90*

Birch, J., 91*
Blackbourn, Joesph, 23, 29
Blair and Company, 30
Blair Field, 69
Blanchet, Phylis, 83*
Bland, Sharon, 81*
Blind Charlie's Freighting, 62*
Blundell, Wilfred, 90*
Boer War, 91*
Bond, Mary, 83*
Bone, A., 91*
Boot Lake, 97*
Boothroyd, Winnifred, 101*
Boston Bar Creek, 12
Boston Bar, 62
Boulanger, L.F., 91*
Boulanger, Mr., 81*
Boyd, Mrs. Percy, 90*
Boyd, P., 35*
Boyden, Noah, 94*
Bradbent, Mrs., 103*
Bradley, W.L., 91*
Brash, G.M., 50*
Breaking camp, 11*
Bresnick, ? , 102*
Brewster, N., 92*
Brigade Lake, 12
Brigade Trails, 10-13*
Brisson, Albert, 81*
British Columbia, 1, 15
British Territory, 12
Brolin, Eric, 79*
Brolin, Gus, 58*
Brolin, Nelson, 79*
Brookmere, 58*, 65
Brown, Dave, 51*
Brown, Jim, 94*

Bryant, Leslie, 42
Bryant, Nellie, 42
Busk, J.L., 91*

C

Cameron, Gordon, 88*
Campbell, Hugh, 88*
Canada, 69
Canadian Pacific Railway, 38, 49, 54, 65*, 71
Canford Mills, 31, 57*, 58
Canford Public School, 78*
Canford, 31*, 57, 60*, 79
Capps, 41
Cariboo Goldfields, 23
Carr, Margaret, 90*
Carr, Percy, 84*
Carrington, Arthur, 28*, 103*
Carrington, Bobby, 103*
Carrington, Dorothy, 103*
Carrington, Gertie, 103*
Carrington, Laurie, 103*
Carrington, Mrs. A., 103*
Carrington, Thomas, 23*
Cartwright, Harold, 95*
Cassidy, Bella, 102*
Cassidy, Bill, 94*, 95*
Cassidy, Donna, 80*
Cassidy, J., 92*
Cassidy, Johnny, 94*, 95*
Catholic Sacred Heart Church, 85*
Cenotaph, 91*, 102*
Central Hall, 98*
Chapman Street, 34
Chapman, Jack, 77*, 103*
Chapman, James, 22, 24, 25*, 40, 50
Chapman, John, 76
Chapman, Mrs. Jim, 103*
Chapperon Lake, 15, 39
Charlie, (Blind) Cultus, 62*
Charters Street, 34
Charters, Harry, 42

Charters, John, 23*, 32, 41
Charters, Robert, 29
Charters, William, 23, 24, 25*, 32, 41, 50, 76
Chelahilsa, Chief John, 89*
Childs, George, 66*
Chipp, John, 83
Christianson, G.S., 91*
City Hotel, 74*
Clapperton Ranch, 39
Clapperton, George, 22, 23*
Clapperton, John, 21, 22, 23*, 27*, 28
Clark, Dick, 93*
Clark, Jack, 24, 25*, 39;
Clark, Kelly, 88*, 95*
Clark, Winney, 39
Clay Bluffs, 66*
Cleasby Street, 34
Cleasby, Henry S. (Harry), 24, 25*, 40, 46*, 50, 79
Cleasby, Joe, 46*
Cleasby, Mrs. Harry, 103*
Clemens, Della, 90*, 93*
Clinton, 48
Coal Gulley, 49
Cochenour, R., 91*
Coldwater Coal Co., 49
Coldwater Hotel, 73*
Coldwater Reserve, 16
Coldwater River, 32, 40, 49, 50, 77, 97*
Coldwater School, 78, 81
Coldwater Valley, 56*, 85
Collett Ranch, 40*
Collett, Alfred, 24, 25*
Collett, Allan, 92*, 94*, 95*, 102*
Collett, Charles, 47
Collett, Edgar, 47
Collett, Harry, 40*, 43*
Collett, Jack, 40*
Collett, John H., 40
Collett, Mrs. Harry, 90*
Collins, A. "Scotty", 94*

Collins, G., 91*
Connor, J., 91*
Conper, Bob, 51*
Cook, L., 91*
Cook, Tom, 102*
Cooper, Bob, 93*
Coquihalla Pass, 12, 65
Coquihalla River, 12
Coquihalla Trail, 38
Coquihalla, 64, 82
Corkle, Jean, 93*
Corkle, Vernon, 41*
Cottett, Mrs. Charlie, 90*
Courtney Lake Cow Camp, 40*, 42*
Cousins, Ed, 103*
Coutlee Avenue, 34
Coutlee Hotel, 70
Coutlee's Blacksmith Shop, 30
Coutlee, 24, 30*, 46*, 49, 51*, 63*, 70
Coutlee, Alexander, 24, 25, 30, 40
Coutlee, Alma, 77*
Coutlee, Joe, 40*, 42*
Coutlee, Ranger, 43*
Cowboy Race, 99*
Coy Cup Winners, 94*
Coyle, (Lower Nicola), 54
Crabtree, Ted, 78*
Craigmont Mines, 54*, 55*
Cranna, Bill, 95*
Crompton, W., 47
Cross, Henry, 97*
Cum Cloups (Kamloops), 10
Cummings, Jimmy, 78*
Cummings, Margorie, 78*
Curling, 95*
Curnow, Dick, 40*
Curnow, Geoff, 41*
Curnow, Gordon, 41*
Curnow, Leslie, 40*
Curnow, Richard, 31
Curnow, Thomas, 24, 25*, 40

D

Dallas, Walter, 93*
Dalley, Edwin, 21*, 85
Dalton, J., 92*
Dalton, J.A., 91*
Dalton, M., 92*
Davidson, R., 91*
Davis Ranch, 39
Davis, Gary, 78*
Davis, Henry, 39
Davis, Wilbur, 39
Dennison, Jack, 75*
Dewolf & Ham, 58*
Diamond Jubilee, 100*
Diamondvale Coal Mines, 49, 50, 53*
Diamondvale Store, 36*
Dobbie, Bill, 88*
Dobbie, Tom, 93*
Dodd's (place), 44*
Dodding, Bart, 90*, 103*
Dodding, Bob, 103*
Dodding, David, 77*, 103*
Dodding, Fred, 90*
Dodding, Harriet, 90*
Dodding, John, 77*, 90*
Dodding, Johnnie, 103*
Dodding, Mary, 77*, 103*
Dodding, Mr. Sr., 103*
Dodding, Mrs. Sr., 103*
Dodding, Willie, 77*, 103*
Doren, Slim, 42*
Douglas Lake Cattle Company, 39*;
founded by, 42, 85
Douglas Lake, 15, 16, 42, 44*, 85
Driard Hotel, 28, 63*, 70*
Dryborough, W., 91*
Drying Fish, 4*
Dunlop, ? , 102*
Dunlop, Inez, 83*
Dunlop, Johnny, 102*
Dunnigan, Bernard, 88*
Dunnigan, Frank, 88*
Dunnigan, John, 93*
Dunnigan, W.J., 91*

E

Early Automobiles, 67*, 68*
Early Mining Equipment, 53*
Early Native Implements, 6*
Earnshaw, Byron, 23
Earnshaw, Herman, 40*
Eastwood, I., 35*, 46*
Electric Locomotive, 55*
Ellingson, Blondie, 40*
Ellis, Dr., 49
Ellis, Jim, 95*
England, 41
Ewart, Derry, 88*
Ewart, Greta, 83*

F

Fairfoull, Bob, 88*
Fairley, Bill, 93*, 102*
Fairley, David, 93*
Fairley, J., 102*
Fairley, Jean, 83*
Fairley, L.F., 91*
Fairley, Ray, 88*
Farr, Mr., 81*
Farr, Mrs., 81*
Fensom, George, 27
Ferguson, R., 91*
Fink, Ben, 43*
First Airplane, 69*
First Court House, 86*
First Hearse, 66*
First High School Class, 80*
First May Day Celebration, 101*
First Merritt School Class of 1908, 79*
First Post Office, 82*
First School, 80*
Fisher, H.C., 91*
Flower Cottage, 86*
Forks of Nicola, 22
Forks, The, 22, 24, 30, 32, 33
Forksdale, 32, 33, 50, 52
Forsythe H.E., 79
Fort Hope, 12
Fort Okanagan, 10-11
Fraser River, 12
Fraser, Berta, 78*
Fraser, Ernest, 79
Fraser, Jack, 78*
Fraser, Mr., 103*
Fraser, Peter, 78

G

Garcia Street, 34, 87
Garcia, Celia, 77*
Garcia, Frank, 36*
Garcia, George Jr., 80*
Garcia, Jesus, 23, 24, 25*, 32, 39, 41, 85
Garcia, Pat, 80*
Gardner, Gerry, 81*
Gardners, 41
Garthwaites, 39
Gavelin, ? , 90*
Gavelin, Elin, 80*
Gavelin, Ernie, 88*
Gavelin, Mrs. Eric, 47
Gay, Mrs. Fred, 90*
Geater, Isabell, 93*
George Fensom Mill, 56
Gerrard, Ellen, 90*
Gerrard, Sam, 46*, 102*
Gilderdale, Mr., 103*
Gillespie, Bill, 46*
Gillis, Dr. Austin, 83
Gillis, Dr. J.J., 46, 47, 69, 83, 84*
Gilmore, John, 22
Godison, Alf, 24, 25*
Goldman, Charles S., 39
Gordon, Alex, 24, 25*; 31
Gordon, G., 54*
Graduating Class of 1959, 81*
Graduation Class of 1952, 80*

Grand Hotel, 74, 75*
Grandbois, Gary, 80*
Grandbois, Mrs., 80*
Grandbois, Russell, 80*
Granite Avenue, 34, 37, 87
Grant, J., 102*
Grasslands Hotel, 74
Greaves, David, 93*
Greaves, Joseph Blackbourne, 39*
Greenwood, Jack, 88*
Greig, Harold, 96*
Grimmett, Fred, 101*
Grimmett, M.L., 35*
Guichon, Gerard, 39
Guichon, Johnny, 39*, 40*
Guichon, Joseph A., 71
Guichon, Joseph, 24*, 39, 47, 69, 71, 85
Guichon, Mrs. Joseph, 71
Guichon, Pierre, 39
Guichons, 29, 39, 44*, 46

H

Haddad, Joe, 93*
Hallinan, Bill, 93*
Hallinan, George, 52*, 94*
Hallinan, Peggy, 93*
Hamilton Brothers, 43
Hamilton Corrals, 40*
Hamilton, Jim, 43
Hamilton, John, 43
Hamilton, Robert, 24, 43
Hanna, Dick, 90*
Hanna, Tom, 40, 90*
Hardiman, Jeff, 90*
Hardiman, Lyle, 103*
Hardy, Archie, 95*
Hardy, J.T., 91*
Hardy, Mrs. Archie, 90*
Harrower, J., 91*
Hauling Logs, 57*, 61*
Hendry, John, 48
Heron Brothers, 46*

Heron, Bob, 46
Heron, Jim, 46
Heron, Tom, 46
Hetcher, Herb, 60*
Hill, Frank, 93*
Hobson, J.A., 91*
Hodgson, Blondy, 51*
Hogan, Jim, 75*, 94*
Hogg, A., 91*
Hogg, A.J., 91*
Hogg, Bobbie, 102*
Hogg, D., 91*
Hogg, Donald, 102*
Hoggan, Alexander, 75*
Hoggan, Andrew, 74, 75*
Hoggan, Christina, 74, 75*
Home Guard Lower Nicola, 90*
Hooper, Bob, 88*
Hooshum Ridge, 46
Hope, 12, 38
Hotel Merritt, 72*
Houston, W.A., 91*
Howse, Albert E., 24, 25*, 27*, 28, 33, 87
Hudson's Bay Company, 11-13
Hunter, Allan, 78*
Hunter, Bill, 68
Hunter, Doreen, 80*
Hunter, Flo, 103*
Hunter, Joanne, 78*
Hurdle Race, 99*
Hyland Hall, 79, 85
Hynd, P., 91*

I

Immaculate Conception Church, 85
Ingleby, Edith, 90*
Innes, Bill, 95*
Interior Salish, 1-9; 14-20
Iron Mines Ltd., 49, 50
Irwin, Archie, 77
Isitt, Charles, 93*
Isitt, George, 37*, 93*, 97*

Isitt, Jack, 97*
Isitt, Mrs. George, 37*

J

Jackson Building, 37*
Jackson, Archie, 35*, 86
Jacques, 10-11
James, Ralph, 78*
James, Walter, 78*
Japanese, 55
Jenny, 14*
Jobling, Florence, 90*
Johnson, Bob, 103*
Johnson, Mrs. Bob, 103*
Johnson, Perry, 103*
Johnson, R., 29
Johnston, Perry, 77*
Jones, E.W., 91*
Jones, R., 92*
Josephson, Bruce, 80*
Josephson, Mrs., 90*

K

Kamloops, 12, 63, 69, 71, 95
Kearns, Paddy, 88*
Keehne, Allan, 80*
Keehne, Rodney, 80*
Keekwillie, 2*
Kennedy, Myrtle, 101*
Kettle Valley Railway, 57, 65*
Kiernan, Ken, 54*
King Annie, 79*
King, Del, 24, 25*
King, F., 91*
King, Mona, 79*
Kinnear, Jim, 88*
Kinny, Mr., 48*, 52*
Kinvig, Ed, 90*
Kirby, Mr., 71
Koller, W.J., 91*
Kootenays, 65
Korean War, 91*

Kwolalp, 9*

L

Lacrosse Team, 94*
Ladies Race, 99*
Lake View Fox Farm, 47*
Lambert, Thomas W., 83
Langley, Barbara, 81*
Langstaff, Dorothy, 101*
Langstaff, Glennie, 101*
Lauder Ranch, 41*
Lauder, John, 41
Lauder, Joseph Dixon, 28*, 41
Lauder, Joseph William (Joe), 41*
Lauder, William H., 41
Lauders, (Family), 39
Lawrence, Mable, 80*
Le Jeune, Father, 16*, 84, 85
Leese, John, 51*
Lettice, Mrs., 103*
Lettice, Robert, 22, 27
Lindbergh, Avard, 78*
Lindbergh, Clayton, 78*
Lindbergh, Delnor, 78*
Lindbergh, Marion, 78*
Lindley, David, 77*
Lindley, Dorothy, 77*
Lindley, Henry, 22 , 103*
Lindsay, W., 91*
Logan Lake, 97*
Long, Ken, 90*
Lower Nicola Picnic, 103*
Lower Nicola School District, 79
Lower Nicola School, 77*, 78*
Lower Nicola, 22, 31*; 32, 33, 41, 54, 70, 78, 85, 99
Ludwig, Fritz, 41
Lundbaum, A.W., 23
Lytton, 48, 62

M

Mamette Lake School, 78*

Mamette Lake, 24, 39, 41
Manning, John, 31
Maranatha School, 81
Marshall, Mrs., 47
Martin, E., 94*
Martin, Ted (Capt.), 88*
Martin, Victor, 94*
Matthews Ranch, 39
Maxwell, Jim, 88*
Mayon, Zella, 90*
McCoid, R., 91*
McCrieght, Olive, 90*
McDermott, James P., 84*
McDermott, Mary (Angstadt), 84*
McDiarmid, Neil, 54*
McDonald, Archibald, 11
McDonald, Johnny, 79*
McDougal, A.F., 91*
McDougall, Jerry, 78*
McDougall, Lottie, 78*
McGee, J.C., 91*
McGinnis, Billy, 87*
McGoran, Andrew, 57
McGregor, Dr., 103*
McGregor, L.B., 24, 25*
McGuire, J.D., 83
McInnis, Fred, 103*
McInnis, Mildred, 103*
McInnis, Mrs. Dan, 103*
McInnis, Pearl, 103*
McIntyre, W., 73
McIvor, D.P., 91*
McIvor, W.A., 91*
McKitrick, Bell, 77*, 103*
McKitrick, Josie, 103*
McLeod Lake, 12
McLeod Ranch, 42
McLeod, Delores, 42*,
McLeod, Gordon, 42
McLeod, Joyce, 80*
McLeod, Lee, 80*
McLeod, Monica, 80*

McLeod, Norman (Scotty), 42*
McMillan, N., 35*
McNaulty, J., 91*
McStay, Frank, 93*, 95*
Mealtime, 20*
Meeker, Henry, 57, 58*
Meeker, L., 92*
Megaw, W.R., 29
Menzies, J.A., 35*, 79
Merritt Brewery, 37
Merritt City Hall, 34*
Merritt Court House, 36*
Merritt Fox Ranch, 47
Merritt Funeral Chapel, 86*
Merritt Herald, The, 33
Merritt High School, 92*, 93*
Merritt Post Office, 37*
Merritt Railway Station, 65*
Merritt School District, 79
Merritt Secondary School Staff Of 1959, 81*
Merritt Stampede, 100*
Merritt, (Forksdale), 33, 34
Merritt, 22, 23, 32*;
Merritt, City Hall, 36
Merritt, Father of, 38*
Merritt, Hotel, 75*, 79, 80*, 81*, 82*, 83*
Merritt, move to, 84, 85, 87, 88*
Merritt, Nicola Brewery, 41*, 47*, 64*, 65*
Merritt, telephones, 97*, 100*, 104*
Merritt, William Hamilton, 33, 34*, 49
Methodist Church, 85, 86
Mickle, Florin, 21, 23
Mickle, Mrs. Wheeler, 21*
Mickle, Mrs., 103*
Mickle, Wheeler, 21*
Midday Creek, 58*
Middlesboro Colliery, 50*
Middlesboro, 49*, 50*, 51
Mill Creek Reserve, 17*
Mill Creek, 27, 56
Millar, Issac, 47

Miller, Scotty, 42*
Mills, Joan, 93*
Mitchell, G., 91*
Mooney, Miss, 77*
Moore Family, 39
Moore, Benjamin, 22
Moore, J.N., 94*
Moore, John Pearcy, 22*
Moore, John Sr., 22
Moore, Joseph, 22*
Moore, Margaret, 22
Moore, Samuel, 22*, 23
Moore, Violette, 22*
Morrissey, Jack, 41
Morrissey, Leo, 80*, 81*, 87*, 92*
Moyes, Donna, 81*
Moyes, Mrs. Pete, 90*
Muir, George, 22, 24
Munro, Dan, 68*, 86   35
Munroe, Gordon, 40
Murphy, Michael MacMahon, 29, 83
Murray Lake, 46
Murray United Church, 23, 56, 85*
Murray, George, 103*
Murray, Rev. George, 85
Murray, W., 91*

N
N'tasasha, 17*
Napier Lake, 12
Nash, J.F., 91*
Nash, Mable, 79*
Native Weaponry, 7*
Neale, Ed, 90*
Neilson, Jim, 94*, 95*
Nelson, Frank, 90*
Newkirk, Charles M., 24, 25*
Nicklin, Betty, 80*
Nicklin, Carol, 80*
Nicklin, Grace, 80*
Nicol, H., 91*
Nicola (Upper), 22, 26*, 29, 64*, 68*, 70,

77-86, 95
Nicola (Upper), the settlement, 33, 47*, 38, 49, 56, 63*
Nicola Avenue, 33, 34, 36*, 72, 75*, 86
Nicola Courthouse, 27*
Nicola Herald, The, 33*, 71
Nicola Indian Reserve, 16
Nicola Lake School, 78
Nicola Lake, 1*, 12, 15, 21, 33, 39, 66*, 82, 84
Nicola Livery, Feed & Sale Stables, 63*
Nicola Pine Mills, 57*, 58, 58, 60
Nicola River, 4*, 31, 32, 77
Nicola School District, 79
Nicola School, 76*, 78
Nicola Stock Ranch, 39
Nicola Valley Advocate, The, 33
Nicola Valley Brewery, 37*
Nicola Valley Christian School, 81
Nicola Valley Coal & Coke Co., 49*, 50*, 51*
Nicola Valley General Hospital, 83*
Nicola Valley Meat Market Piggery, 46*
Nicola Valley School of Nursing, 83
Nicola Valley, 1, 2*, 11-14*, 21-24, 29, 33, 38,
Nicola Valley, 48, 60-69*, 71, 76, 82, 85, 87, 102*
Nicolas, Chief (Nicola), 11, 14, 27
Nicomen, 62
Nisbet, Helen, 81*
Nisbet, J., 92*, 94*
Nisbet, Joan, 81*
NMV Lumber, 61

O
O' Rourke, Edward, 29
O' Rourke, Richard, 29
Offley, Constable, 87*
Okanagan Tribe, 1
Okanagan, 11, 65
Old Hessy, 11*

Oldham, Steve, 97*
Orchard, Bert, 69*
Otter Creek Valley, 12
Our Lady of Lourdes, 85
Ovington, John, 93*
Ovington, Larry, 81*
Ovington, M., 91*
Ovington, Matt, 88*

P
Pacific Fur Company, 10
Pack horses, 11*
Page, Edith, 79*
Page, William, 79*
Palmer, William, 24, 78
Pankute, 17*
Patchetts, 59*
Paterson, J., 91*
Paul, J., 91*
Pearse, A.W., 83
Peers Creek, 12
Peers, Henry, 12
Peterie, Myrna, 78*
Petit, George, 27, 28
Petrie, Tom, 94*
Phillips, S., 92*
Pie, Menetta, 103*
Pie, Mrs., 103*
Pie, Rev., 103*
Pierce, Teddy, 51*
Pinecrest Gold Mine, 54
Pioneer Hotel, (Coutlee), 70
Podunk Creek, 12
Poole, S., 91*
Pooley Family, 46
Pooley Hall, 28
Pooley Ranch, 41*
Pooley, Alice, 41
Pooley, Dorothy, 83*
Pooley, Jim, 41
Pooley, William John, 41*
Pooley, William, 28, 41*, 85

Post Meat Market, 37*
Potatoes Illahee, 22, 66*
Potts, J., 60*
Priest Avenue, 83
Priest, Harry, 33, 35*, 95*
Priest, Mrs. (Lily), 79*
Prince Edward Island, 47
Princeton, 63, 65, 69
Prospect, The, 52*
Purvis, H., 91*

Q

Queenie, 31; Woodward's dog
Quilchena Avenue, 33, 34, 36*; 73, 105*
Quilchena Creek, 12
Quilchena Hotel, 71*;
Quilchena Store, 29*, 39
Quilchena, 16, 21, 29, 39, 41, 47*, 70, 79, 85, 95
Quinville Homestead, 39

R

Rankin, Mr., 37
Ransom, Dorothy, 101*
Ransom, Ena, 80*
Ransom, Howard, 95*
Red Cross Workers, 90*
Reid, F. A., 35*
Reid, Gertrude, 81*
Rex Theater, 102*
Rey Ranch, 39
Rice Bros. Circus, 100*
Richard, Mr., 103*
Richard, Mrs., 103*
Richardson, Eddie, 78*
Richardson, John, 78*
Richardson, Margaret, 78*
Riley, Bill, 87*
Riley, Fred, 103*
Riley, George, 87*
Riley, Jack, 87*
Riley, Mrs., 103*

Riley, Rosmond, 93*
Riley, W., 103*
River Ranch, 39, 41*
Robb, Alexander, 21
Robin Hood Play, 77*
Robinson Brothers Farm, 41
Rodgers, Tom, 88*
Roi.pellst, Alice, 9*
Roi.pellst, Amy, 9*
Roi.pellst, Chief Johnny, 9*
Roi.pellst, Sinsimtko, 9*
Root Digger, 5*
Rose, Guy, 39, 71
Ross, Alexander, 10-11, 12*
Ryan, Patrick, 24

S

Salmo, 54
Samuel, Archie, 93*
Sanders Fried Chicken, 105*
Sanderson, Tom, 88*
Satchie, Paul, 85
Saunders Field, 69
Saunders, Mrs., 81*
Schindler, Joe, 90*
Schover, Homer, 90*
Scobie, J., 91*
Scott, Robert, 78
Second World War Forestry Corps, 88*
Service, J., 91*
Shrimpton, Fred, 40*
Shulus Reserve Cowboys, 15*
Shulus, 85
Shuswap Tribe, 1
Shuttleworth, A., 91*
Shuttleworth, Myrtle, 80*
Sickman, George, 40*
Siderfin, John, 78*
Silver Fox Farm, 47*
Similkameen Valley, 29
Simpson and Cranna, 37*
Simpson, J., 54*

Singleton, R.C., 91*
Skidding Logs, 61*
Sleigh Runner, 66*
Smith, Alfred, 77*, 103*
Smith, Bob, 57*
Smith, Conston, 103*
Smith, Dick, 57*
Smith, Elaine, 81*
Smith, James M., 24, 25*, 31
Smith, Jimmie, 103*
Smith, Mable, 57*
Smith, Mrs. Jim, 103*
Smith, Olive, 77*, 80*, 83*, 103*
Smith, Selma, 83*
Smulot, Joesph, 24, 25*
Snider, Billy, 103*
Soloman, Sid, 103*
Sonora, Mexico, 23
Sowerby, E., 91*
Sowerby, Mrs., 90*
Sowoqua Creek, 12
Sparks, Jack, 90*
Spences Bridge, 38, 49, 63, 65*, 69, 83
Spius Creek, 57
Spring Street, 37
St. John's Baptist Church, 85
St. Michael's Anglican Church, 85
St. Nichola's Church, 85
St. Paul's Church, 85
Starrett, Birdie, 103*
Starrett, Eleanor, 103*
Starrett, Mr., 103*
Steffens Ranch, 41
Steffens, Allan, 78*
Steffens, Carroll, 41
Steffens, Dick, 41
Steffens, Frank, 41
Steffens, Fred, 41
Steffens, Henry (Harry), 41
Steffens, Jim, 41
Steffens, Larry, 78*
Steffens, Pat, 78*, 81*

Steffens, Pauline, 103*
Steffens, Rupert, 41
Steffens, Tom, 41
Stelmock, Alex, 94*
Stemwick, Martin, 24
Sterling, Fred, 81*
Steward, Mrs., 103*
Steward, Nat, 103*
Stump Lake, 79
Stoyoma, 46
Summer Range, 97*
Summer Shelters, 3*
Sunshine Orchestra, 102*
Super-Valu, 36*
Sutton, Dr. Alfred Martin, 83
Swan, Sandy, 24, 25*
Swarts, Thomas, 24, 25*

T

Tarzwell, Doreen, 80*
Taylor, Robert, 81*
Teit, Inga, 83*
Teit, Sigurd, 97*
TEkwitlixkEn, 9*
Ten Mile Creek, 52*, 77
Tessier, Marian, 40
Tetlenitsa, Chief John, 9*
Thibideau, Johnny, 79*
Thompson Indians, 1, 2*, 7*
Thompson River Post, 14
Thompson River, 11
Thompson Valley, 12
Thompson, Alex, 93*
Thompson, W.P., 91*
Thompsons, (sheep ranchers), 46
Thomson, Charles W., 39
Tilamoose, T., 91*
Tillery, Ed, 44*

Tolko Industries, 61, 69*
Tolko Mill, 58
Tommage, W., 91*
Trinity United Church, 85
Tulameen Rd., 10*, 12
Turnbull, Bob, 81*
Turner, Richard W., 22
Tutill, Dr. George M., 83, 103*
Tutill, Mrs., 103*

U

United States, 12
Upper Nicola, (See Nicola)

V

Valley Natives, 15*, 16*, 17*, 18*, 19*
Valnicola Hotel, 74
Vancouver, 49, 51*, 83, 87
Vicar, Miss, 83*
Victoria Day, 99
Voght Street, 34, 73, 105*
Voght, Lena, 79*
Voght, Tena, 79*
Voght, William, 23*, 24, 25*, 32, 36*,
Voght, William, 41; 50, 85

W

Wade, Jenny, 79*
Wade, Ruth, 101*
Wade, Viola, 93*
Walker, Bob, 88*
Walker, E., 91*
Walters, Jackie, 43*
Ward, William C., 39
Watson, Carl, 78*
Watson, Karen, 78*
Weir, 4*
Weyerhaeuser, 61
Whitaker, Bob, 90*

Whitaker, Joe, 90*
Whiteford, John, 41
Wilcox, J., 91*
Williams, Dr. Cyrill S., 83
Williams, Mrs. Tommy, 90*
Willow Heights Ranch, 42
Wilson, Johnny, 24, 25*
Winney Ranch, 39
Winnie, Gordon, 103*
Winnie, Harry, 103*
Woods, S.J., 70
Woodward Settlement, 77
Woodward, Bertha, 77*, 103*
Woodward, C.N., 39
Woodward, Chrissie, 77*, 103*
Woodward, Clarence, 103*
Woodward, Frank, 103*
Woodward, Fred, 77*, 90*, 103*
Woodward, Grace, 103*
Woodward, Harvey, 22, 24, 76, 103*
Woodward, Henry, 22*, 103*
Woodward, Jennie, 77*, 103*
Woodward, Jim, 103*
Woodward, Marcus, 24, 31, 70, 103*
Woodward, Marion, 103*
Woodward, Melvin, 31*
Woodward, Mrs. Marcus, 103*
Woodward, Myrtle, 103*
Woodward, Norman, 64*, 103*
Woodward, Ramona, 103*
Woodward, Thomas, 22, 24
World War 1, 89*, 91*, 92*
World War 2, 89, 91*
Wright, H.P., 91*

X

XaxalExkEn, 9*

Merritt & the Nicola Valley:

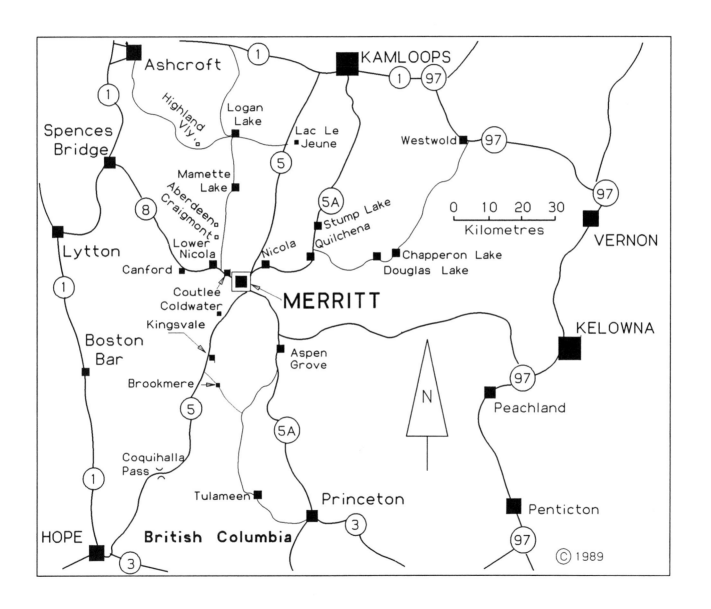